ADVANCE PRAISE

"*Your Grass Is Greener* is an essential guide for anyone looking to transform their life for the better. Jason Silver's practical advice and relatable examples provide powerful tools for improving communication, decision-making, job satisfaction, and success. This book is a game-changer for professionals seeking to enhance their effectiveness and enjoyment at work without changing jobs. A must-read for those committed to personal and professional growth!"

—JAY ROSENZWEIG, CEO and Founder of Rosenzweig & Company

"Too often, we try to fix internal struggles with external solutions and wonder why it doesn't work. *Your Grass Is Greener* is a timely reminder that true fulfillment begins with self-awareness and intentional action. Silver's insights give us the right tools for the job and teach us how to use them to cultivate a greener, more vibrant landscape right where we are."

—HENNA PRYOR, Author of *Good Awkward*

"*Your Grass Is Greener* offers the most actionable work advice I've read in a long time. I've led teams both big and small, and the lessons Silver shares cover the most common professional challenges from a completely new perspective. His anecdotes pull you in, and the takeaways are applicable where they're needed most, your everyday work. *Your Grass Is Greener* is an operating manual for a better way to work, no matter what work you do."

—SAM SEBASTIAN, VP and Country Manager, Google

"This is the kind of book you'll want to buy multiples of to share with the people you care about. The highest performing, most magnetic people I've worked with know how to get things done while always seeming to be enjoying themselves the most along the way. I could never put my finger on the secret sauce until *Your Grass Is Greener*. Silver's tactics provide an actionable guide for a better way to work—having a bigger impact all while enjoying yourself more along the way."

—AARON ZIFKIN, Managing Director, Lyft;
Regional Director, Airbnb

"*Your Grass Is Greener* is a clear-minded operating manual for finding joy and fulfillment *through* your work. Jason Silver delivers powerful stories and evidence-based tools that remind us of what we so easily forget: you don't have to abandon your life to transform how you live."

—SUNEEL GUPTA, Bestselling Author of
*Everyday Dharma: 8 Essential Practices for
Finding Success and Joy in Everything You Do*

"This is the most unique blend of performance and fulfillment I've ever read. The stories in *Your Grass Is Greener* are captivating, and the tactics are immediately actionable. If you want to work hard and achieve a lot, without paying for it with your life outside of the office, this will become your go-to guide. I can't wait to share the book with my entire team!"

—KRISTIN LANGENFELD, CEO and Cofounder, GoodBuy Gear

"*Your Grass Is Greener* is a must-read for anyone who wants to get more joy—and success—from their job and life. Learn how to be more productive, make better decisions, and achieve more than you thought possible. Silver shares strategies and tactics that you can implement today to have better results tomorrow."

—JANET BANNISTER, Managing Partner, Staircase Ventures

"*Your Grass Is Greener* is a brilliant handbook for anyone looking to feel more fulfilled at work. The pragmatic tips and practical examples are backed by science and proven to work in companies of any size. I've seen first-hand the impact these methods can have on people's happiness and effectiveness at work. I highly recommend you read it and revisit it often whenever you hit a wall at work. You may be a lot closer than you think to your dream job."

—STEVE IRVINE, Founder and CEO, integrate.ai

"With the perfect mix of humor, research, and real-life examples, *Your Grass Is Greener* goes well beyond workplace buzzwords and quick tips that are often impossible to put into practice. Throughout the book, Silver shares practical, achievable steps for increasing your productivity and happiness at work. Whether you're looking for ways to accomplish even more or struggling with your career satisfaction overall, this book will give you plenty to think about—and the tools you need to turn those thoughts into action!"

—MEGAN SERES, Managing Director, Accenture

"*Your Grass Is Greener* combines practical lessons with systems and operating models that will help you excel in the office and at home. This book is perfect for leaders and employees alike, making workplace lessons feel more fun through anecdotes covering everything from Springsteen to space travel. Using Silver's actionable exercises, you'll become The Boss at work and in life, rocketing yourself to new heights."

—ALEX BAKER, Managing Partner, Relay Ventures

"*Your Grass Is Greener* offers practical, no-nonsense advice for anyone looking to up their game at work."

—LAURA GASSNER OTTING, Bestselling Author of *Wonderhell* and *Limitless*

YOUR
GRASS
IS
GREENER

YOUR GRASS IS GREENER

USE WHAT YOU HAVE
GET WHAT YOU WANT
AT WORK AND IN LIFE

JASON SILVER

IDEAPRESS
PUBLISHING

WASHINGTON, DC

IDEAPRESS
PUBLISHING

Ideapress Publishing | www.ideapresspublishing.com

All trademarks are the property of their respective companies.

Cover Design: David Fassett
Interior Design: Jessica Angerstein

Cataloging-in-Publication Data is on file with the Library of Congress.

Hardcover ISBN: 978-1-64687-166-7

Special Sales
Ideapress books are available at a special discount for bulk purchases for sales promotions and premiums, or for use in corporate training programs. Special editions, including personalized covers, a custom foreword, corporate imprints, and bonus content, are also available.

1 2 3 4 5 6 7 8 9 10

For my sister Rachel.

CONTENTS

PREFACE

"Hi, you have two guests staying at your hotel, the Silvers."

The concierge says, "I'm sorry, sir. We can't talk about our guests."

"Right." I pause, unsure of what to say. "I really need to reach my parents. I've called them multiple times, but I think they've turned their phones off."

No reply.

I reiterate, "I know they're staying at your hotel. I just don't know what room. How can I get in touch with them?"

Thankfully, he replies, "What's your name?"

"Jason Silver. I'm their son. I *really* need to reach them. *Please.*"

I imagine he hears the strain in my voice and says, "I'll put you through."

I'm standing in the corner of a dark, unoccupied patient room in the ER at Sunnybrook Hospital in Toronto. It's around 9 or 10 p.m. I really can't remember the exact time. I do remember the noise. There's a constant hum and a never-ending beeping of machines monitoring patients, in some cases keeping them alive altogether. The PA system blares to life every two to three minutes, alerting the medical staff to some form of crisis. Code blues sound particularly bad. Nurses rush every which way, and although I'm sure their team is on top of things, the environment looks and feels like chaos to me.

My sister Rachel is unaware of the noise. Thankfully, she's finally asleep after hours of being poked, prodded, and scanned. Earlier that morning, on her doctor's advice, she'd walked into the hospital and was immediately rushed to an emergency room and a battery of tests. Now that she's asleep, I sneak out to that unoccupied room to call my parents, who are away on vacation.

I'm about to have to put together the hardest few sentences of my life.

I hear a click as the hotel concierge connects the call to my parents' room. I'm exhausted and confused. Somehow I have to break the news to my mom and dad that doctors suspect my sister has a very aggressive, very late-stage form of cancer. How the hell do I say this? What do I even tell them? I don't really know anything yet myself. Should I even be calling them? There's nothing they can do at the moment. They're not even in the country.

My dad picks up. "It's Jason," he says to my mother. I hear her gasp from across the room and ask what's happening with Rachel. She knew right away that something was seriously wrong. A mother's intuition.

"Well, Dad, I have some hard news..."

I tell them what I know. The phone call ends, and all at once the realization of everything that happened that day hits me. I'm physically sick, but I make it to the bathroom before causing another issue for the busy medical staff to deal with.

This is the beginning of the last chapter of my sister's life and the worst chapter of mine. A few months later, shortly before her thirty-seventh birthday, my sister lost her battle with cancer.

Losing Rachel sent me into a spiral. I fell to pieces, slowly picked them all back up again, and through her death have been learning more about how to better live my own life. I challenged every assumption I had about how I was living and focused on my own well-being more than I ever had before. Over time I started to feel better in life and turned my attention to work. A similar deep dive upended everything I thought I knew about how I was supposed to work, and in the process, helped me find a better way. One that allows me to continue to work hard, but enjoy myself more along the way.

It took me years to get back on my feet. I still have tough days, but Rachel's passing seems to have possessed me with a passion for finding a better way to work and live. I would trade all of the lessons I've learned to bring her back if I could, but I can't, so instead I choose to share them with you. My hope is that by applying what you're about to read, you'll experience the same life-altering benefits I did—without needing a tragedy to bring them about.

Thank you for picking up a copy of my book and giving the tactics within a try. Rachel inspired me to improve so much about my approach to life, particularly when it comes to work, and I'm grateful for the opportunity to pay it forward to you.

Now that the tough stuff is out of the way, let's dive into how you can transform your job into one of the most positive drivers in your life.

Thank you.

INTRODUCTION

To change my life

A bathtub full of near-subzero water challenges me to get in, but all I can do is stare back and wonder, *Why am I doing this?* I'm three weeks into yet another experiment to make my life better. This time, it's cold plunges. I read that spending three minutes every day in freezing water increases your dopamine and that makes you feel better. And I needed to feel better.

A few months after Rachel passed away I started experimenting. What began as a search for anything that could just help me cope grew into a borderline obsession with understanding emotion, happiness, and the role of work in my overall well-being. I read hundreds of books spanning neuroscience, positive and behavioral psychology, philosophy, human evolution, and more. I read more self-help books than I care to admit. I started meditating daily. I tried intermittent fasting. I tried running. Walking. Hanging by my arms. I slept more. Slept less. If you've heard of a way to live a happier, more fulfilled life, there's a good chance I've tried it.

Some experiments turned into habits I still practice today, like therapy and regular meditation. Others like intermittent fasting (which turned into intermittent overeating to make up for the regular hunger) and quitting soap to foster a healthier microbiome didn't stick. (Yes, I still washed my hands; no, I didn't smell quite as bad as you might think; but yes, in retrospect, quitting soap should have been an obvious pass.)

I turned my life into an ongoing experiment in my own positive psychology, which is how I found myself on the losing end of a staring competition with a bathtub. In that moment, I realized that all the experiments I'd tried to make my life better could only accomplish so much. I was feeling better, but I also felt as if I'd plateaued. Then the proverbial light went off over my head.

It's not your life that's the issue. It's where you actually spend most of your time.

How to work—and live—better

Research has shown that enjoying your job isn't just a nice perk. The more you enjoy your work, the better you do at it. You're more creative and you build better relationships with your colleagues too. Studies also show that the joy you feel at your job spills into the rest of your life. When you enjoy your work, you have more energy for everything else. Simply put, working better is the key to unlocking better work and a better life.

WORKING BETTER UNLOCKS **BETTER WORK** AND A **BETTER LIFE.**

If you're like me and you care about your career, you almost certainly have something you'd like to improve about your job. Maybe you love what you do today and are just looking to advance in some way, or your work might be really draining for you and you need a more substantial change. That dream job you've always wanted? It might feel like it's forever out of reach, but it's much closer than you realize. You just need to take an unconventional path to get there.

Too often we're taught to hang our happiness on hitting milestones. You think everything will be better when you land that new project, join a new team, get that promotion you've been working hard for, or jump to a new job entirely. Thinking they had found better jobs elsewhere, millions of people tried this strategy during the Great Resignation and quit the jobs they had. Survey them today and you'll find that rather than relief, eight in ten feel regret. Simply changing what you do is unlikely to lead to lasting improvements for you.

Alternatively, we're told to consider going in the opposite direction and cut back on our careers to free up more time outside of the office. Again, this strategy seems sound until you dig into the details. Millions of quiet quitters, people who take balance to an extreme—

doing the minimum necessary not to get fired—report feeling more stressed than ever at work and that they're struggling in their lives overall. Sure, you can free up your time by cutting back, but doing less at work seems to stress you out more if you have any ambition.

The problem with both of these strategies is that they focus on changing your environment. They rely on "grass is greener" thinking—assuming that all of your problems are situational—and you know how grass is greener stories end. In all but the most toxic situations, when a different environment truly is needed, changing what you work on feels better at first, but before long you wind up right back where you started, with the same stresses and challenges you've always had. This happens because changing what you do rarely addresses the root cause of the most common workplace challenges: how you're working.

YOU DON'T NEED DIFFERENT WORK TO FEEL BETTER, YOU JUST NEED TO **DO THE WORK YOU ALREADY HAVE DIFFERENTLY.**

When you improve your underlying approach to work and the challenges you face in your job, the benefits you feel will compound. The next project, next team, next task you do will all get better because the way you're working overall has improved. That's why the unconventional answer for better work is to focus on *how*. Don't start by assuming you need to change your environment, start with how you're working instead. You'll know for sure that it's time to find something new to do if you've tried to improve how you work and it isn't helping.

The path to lasting improvements is all about your approach day-to-day.

I only figured this out after the personal experiments I had been doing plateaued. I was feeling better outside of the office, so I started looking inside the office, and that's when I realized work wasn't working for me.

Work needed to change, but how?

Back then I was building a company, stressing about payroll and simply enduring the grind. I was accomplishing a lot, but it felt like I was hanging on for dear life. Surviving, not thriving. I always made sure to fit family time in and prioritized a few weeks' vacation every year, but the model was always the same: fill my time and my mind with work and then use the space between all of the projects, people, and planning for "life." I felt like I had to choose between ambition at work or life outside of it.

I regularly struggled to find the right balance. I'd make a big work push at the expense of my life or shortchange my team to spend time elsewhere. I felt great after hitting a big milestone and grumpy anytime I was off target from my goals. I assumed that because of how much I cared about my career and how hard I wanted to work at it, work could have good moments, but on the whole wouldn't be something to truly enjoy—that would come later once I'd "made it." I never questioned why. But I figured there had to be a better way, so I brought my self-experimentation into the office.

This time, I read everything I could get my hands on about organizational psychology, management, leadership, 4-hour workweeks, biographies of successful CEOs, and on and on. I tried to read it all and began testing what I was learning. What happens if I set more goals? What about swearing them off and not setting a single one for an entire year? (Like soap, it turns out goals are good hygiene, and I should have skipped this test too.) I tried working fewer days for longer hours and more days for less. I'm lucky I had a very understanding team at the time.

In all that experimenting, I learned that many of our assumptions about work are fundamentally flawed.

As I experimented more and more, keeping what worked and learning from what didn't, I started having a bigger impact and enjoying myself more along the way. Even more surprising, I felt better across the rest of my life as well. I was learning a better way to work, and in the process, transforming the job I already had into a more positive driver in my life overall.

Work was working for me.

It wasn't long before my colleagues noticed the differences I'd been feeling. When they began asking me about my experiments and incorporating them into their own jobs, I realized I wasn't alone in wanting a better work life.

I'm sure you've questioned what an improvement at work could look like for you. Can you achieve more? Should you even try? Is it possible to enjoy your day-to-day more? Should you stay in the job you have, or find something new? Will the grass truly be any greener elsewhere? Now, more than ever, thoughts like these seem to be top of mind for employees around the world.

Work isn't working

Workplace statistics paint a clear picture: the way we're working today isn't working.

- Productivity is lower than ever.
- About eight in ten people have burned out at least once at their current job.
- Seventy-seven percent of employees feel disengaged from work.
- And the "Great Resignation" and "quiet quitting" have become so popular as to be routinely newsworthy.

If, like so many others, you're struggling at your job today, know that you can turn it around. On the other hand, if you're one of the lucky few feeling good about your job, even small improvements can have a big impact on the rest of your life because of how much time you spend at work. Whether you enjoy your job or not, work still presents us with our biggest—if not our most persistent—hurdles to enjoying life. Even among those doing well at work, a 2023 global survey found that people most commonly reference workplace challenges like too much work, too many hours, and too much stress at the office as the biggest obstacles to improving their well-being overall.

Whatever job you have and however it's going for you today, finding ways to work better will bring you big benefits both at the office and outside of it.

The secret to better work

Work smarter, not harder.

Does anyone even know what that actually means? Are you waking up every day trying to work dumb? No, you're not. The problem isn't you or what you're capable of; it's that no one has ever really explained *how* you're supposed to work smarter. Seemingly wise sayings meant to help you work better sound great until you try to implement them:

- Think outside the box: *Are you trying to constrain your thinking?*
- Believe in yourself: *Is self-doubt that simple to overcome?*
- Focus is the foundation of success: *Do you intentionally get distracted?*
- Move fast: *I have an idea! Why don't we go really slow just for fun?*

Though memorable, most slogans and sayings are light on details about what you're actually supposed to do differently. In all my time helping others improve their work lives, I've found that the same small handful of challenges come up again and again. To name a few, we all get frustrated at constant miscommunications, hate waiting for decisions, want to move faster, feel self-doubt, and are always looking for exciting opportunities everyone else misses.

Despite what you may have been told, you don't need to develop a deep expertise in any one tactic to help you work better. No amount of better prioritization will help you improve your communication. Instead, you can use the skills you already have to make just enough progress across each of the most common workplace challenges. The biggest benefits don't come from going deep in one area. You get the most overall improvement from going shallow, but wider.

YOU DON'T NEED NEW SKILLS TO *WORK BETTER.* YOU CAN **USE THE SKILLS YOU ALREADY HAVE.**

Through the unique, nonobvious insights I learned from my experimentation, I'm going to show you the failures of conventional workplace wisdom on each of the most common workplace challenges. I'll share an unconventional view of the problem itself and provide a practical antidote you can put to work right away.

I've been through countless far-fetched and failed experiments so you don't have to. I'll fast-forward you right to the highest impact tactics that it took me to get there (without the detours through swearing off soap and confusingly working without goals). We'll break down nine of the most impactful tactics for working better across three opportunity areas:

- How to do five days of work in four
  (without working until midnight)
- How to enjoy your day-to-day work more
  (without changing jobs)
- How to progress faster (without waiting for a promotion)

What you'll learn works because each tactic is focused entirely on what you control. No waiting for your boss to approve a new project, spending months interviewing for a "dream job" that may never come, or holding yourself back anymore.

Who the heck am I?

Though I don't want you to simply take my word on the potential of the tactics to come—you should try them and see how they work for you—I do think it might help to tell you more about myself than my background in bathtub-staring competitions.

I'm a multi-time founder of humans (two boys) and a multi-time founder of companies. I've been very lucky to pack a wide breadth of experiences into my career so far. I've seen everything from company creation through to both total collapse and unmitigated global success. Along the way I've had the privilege to lead incredible teams, work with countless others, and learn from some of the best in the business.

I was fortunate to help scale Airbnb in its earlier days and lucky to contribute to the artificial intelligence revolution at my most recent company, integrate.ai. In all that time, I noticed how much I loved helping people enjoy doing the hard things in their lives. Today, I work with a portfolio of founders and their teams on:

- how to build great, lasting businesses that people love to work for
- how to do better and feel better at work
- how to do both of these things using what you already have available to you

My clients are the household names you haven't heard of yet because their companies are in their early stages. Collectively they've achieved a valuation approaching $2 billion—and they're just getting started.

Many of these clients have asked me for the book you're now reading. They've told me how helpful these tactics have been in their lives and in their work. And I'm grateful to them for being willing test subjects in my ongoing experimentation to make work work better.

Grow with what you know

The principles you'll read in this book were developed through hundreds of hours of my own experimentation, and further refined across hundreds more, helping others implement them in their own work lives as well.

This book is a practical guide you can use to improve the work you already have, using skills you also already have. I'll simply show you how to use what you have differently. You may not believe me until you see it for yourself, but if you can talk, you'll be able to try every tactic you're about to read.

Whether you need to turn around a bad situation at your job or already enjoy your work and are looking for ways to do better, what you'll get is a map to show you how to achieve more in less time, with less stress and with less detriment to your overall well-being (and no cold plunges).

This isn't a book to help you rediscover your cosmic purpose or make a career change you'll later regret. It also won't help you slack off and sneak it past your boss. If, on the other hand, you care about your career and are constantly on the hunt for how to work better day-to-day, then read on. I'll show you why you don't need a new job to land your dream job, and how you can transform the job you already have today instead. When you do, work will become one of the most positive drivers in your life overall.

You already have everything you need to get what you want at work and in life.

Let me show you how.

PART 1

How to Do 5 Days of Work in 4 (Without Working until Midnight)

Though common, the biggest workplace slowdowns are all too often overlooked. Once you see them, they become obvious. When you solve them, you take back control of your time.

How would you spend a full day of work every week if you were able to free it up? Would you reinvest it in that important project you never have time to work on? Improve yourself or your job so you can progress faster and enjoy yourself more?

In Part 1, we'll cover three different counterintuitive tactics for doing five days of work in four with no drop in your impact—freeing up to a full day every single week. What you do with your newfound time will be up to you. How to reclaim it is the job of the next three chapters.

UNBLOCK

- **Chapter 1:** Miscommunications are costing you more than you know—eliminating them requires the opposite of better clarifying what you say.
- **Chapter 2:** Trying to get agreement on every decision is wasting your time—doing the opposite will speed up slow decision-making on your team.
- **Chapter 3:** A bug in your brain unknowingly sets you up to work more hours than you need to—the secret to getting more done in less time is the opposite of a to-do list.

Are you a Bruce Springsteen fan? I am, but there was a brief moment when I really wasn't. Let me tell you the story of how The Boss almost blew up my career and, in the process, taught me the most valuable lesson in communication I've ever learned.

THE DAY SPRINGSTEEN NEARLY CRASHED MY CAREER

How to Eliminate Miscommunication

The single biggest problem with communication
is the illusion that it has taken place.

—GEORGE BERNARD SHAW

Note to self: When you royally mess up, don't do it when the NBA, the NHL, Airbnb, and The Boss are all involved. *A Night At* was one of my favorite campaigns we ran at Airbnb. Anyone could enter a competition for a once-in-a-lifetime, one-night, two-day sports double-header sleepover at the Raptors/Maple Leafs home stadium in downtown Toronto. Doug Gilmour, a famous retired Maple Leafs player, would host the winners. They'd take a behind-the-scenes tour, then watch the Leafs game that night from center ice.

Next, they'd be escorted to their very own private Airbnb "home" in the stadium, a corporate box we'd converted to look like a genuine camp cabin, complete with wood paneling and flannel sheets. However, instead of overlooking a lake, it looked over a lake of ice surrounded by 20,000 empty seats. In the morning, our winners would be awakened... Not by the singing of birds, but by the blaring of the stadium-wide goal horn and the antics of Carlton the Bear, the Leafs' team mascot. (At least the bear was still in theme.)

While they slept, the ice was converted into a basketball court in preparation for that night's Toronto Raptors game. After they ate breakfast, they'd tour the Raptors facilities and take part in a pregame shootaround. Then the winners would watch the game from courtside. To this day, I remain jealous that employees couldn't enter the contest.

But there was a much larger problem: Bruce Springsteen.

As you can imagine, there was a lot of work involved in making the *Night At* event happen. Between planning the event itself and negotiating with the NBA, NHL, Leafs, Raptors, and the stadium, there were a lot of moving pieces. We had spent months sorting out all of the details. On our way to what I thought was a meeting to finally sign the contracts, someone on their end mentioned their excitement for the five days they'd locked in for the event.

Uh, do what now?

When they showed me the chosen dates—with the hockey game and basketball game separated by three full days—I nearly fell over. I said what I thought was obvious: "These games need to be on back-to-back nights." I asked, "Why is there a three-day gap?"

"The Springsteen concert needs that long to build up and tear down."

I generally consider myself a Springsteen fan but, in that moment, I wished he'd been born to run somewhere else.

The high cost of miscommunication

Miscommunication in the workplace costs the US economy upward of $1.2 trillion every year. Only sixteen countries have higher GDPs than that staggering number. Let's put that into a perspective that matters in your day-to-day life. At the individual level, workplace miscommunications lead to an estimated loss of 7.47 hours per person per week. Think about that. We all lose nearly a full business day of productivity *every single week*. You might not have a big miscommunication like I had with the *Night At* every week, but smaller miscommunications add up. Fifteen minutes here, twenty minutes there. By the end of the week, the impact is significant. A full day!

Aside from productivity, miscommunicating just feels bad. A recent study showed that most employees (69 percent) can point to a specific, recent miscommunication at work that left them feeling more stressed or anxious. Almost one in four is considering a new job because of miscommunication in the workplace. We're losing our patience and our time.

Consider this as well: When was the last time you recognized a miscommunication in the moment, did nothing about it, and charged ahead regardless? That's probably never happened. You usually don't discover that a costly miscommunication has happened until *after* you've gone down the wrong path, done the wrong work, agreed to the wrong dates, and wasted unnecessary effort and energy. In other words, first you pay the price and only then do you see the wasted effort.

This chapter will help you identify these invisible miscommunications in the moment, *before* you pay the price. By the end—assuming you're not laughing at the irony of my possibly failed attempt to communicate about miscommunication—you'll have a specific tactic to stop all miscommunications before they ever have a chance to start. Your opportunity is immense. If you can reduce your miscommunications in the workplace, you can get back almost an entire workday every single week with no loss to your output. In other words, you'll accomplish five days of work in four.

The problem behind the problem of miscommunication

Understandably, no one wanted to ask Springsteen's people to reschedule. (They don't call him The Boss for nothing.) Finding back-to-back hockey and basketball games was rare. And the stadium's schedule was fully booked at least a year in advance. After months of hard work and excitement for what the *Night At* could be, the deal seemed dead. Some might even say it went "Dancing in the Dark" (though not me, of course).

In hindsight, Bruce was not the problem. The problem was me.

Each element of this multifaceted, multi-organization, heavily-invested-in event had been clear to everyone, but the mission-critical requirement of back-to-back games had been missing from the outset. It wasn't because I'd forgotten to mention that key fact. Rather, I'd made a classic blunder of communication: I assumed others had interpreted my words how I'd intended them to be interpreted.

I'd forgotten one of the most obvious and important rules of communication: different people hear the same words differently. To illustrate this, I play the following game with teams when I'm brought in to help with their communication skills. I ask everyone to bring a piece of paper, close their eyes, and follow these instructions that I read out loud:

1. Fold your sheet of paper in half.

2. Tear off the upper right corner.

3. Fold your paper in half again.

4. Tear off the lower right corner.

5. Fold your paper in half.

6. Tear off the upper left corner.

7. Fold in half a final time.

8. Tear off the lower left corner.

9. Unfold your paper and hold it up.

10. Open your eyes, look at your product, and compare it with the others.

Ten very simple steps. The picture below shows three randomly chosen results from one such test. I could have picked any three and you'd see the same thing. What do you notice?

You got it. They're all different. I've done this exercise countless times and I've *never* seen any two pages look the same. Try it with your friends or your team at work. Every single person hears exactly the same instructions. Every single person produces a different end product. Why does this happen?

The answer is obvious, yet all too often forgotten. We're all different from each other. We all think differently. We all hear things differently. Different people can hear the exact same instructions and produce completely different results. Remember playing Broken Telephone as a kid? We fundamentally can't assume that what we say will be interpreted by others in the way we intend.

Yet we often do just that. We know we're different from one another and that we hear words differently, but we tend to forget this when we're actually communicating with each other. Think about the last time you had to tell someone something important. If you're like most people, you probably spent all of your time figuring out what to say. How much time did you spend confirming that it landed?

More often than not, you get your message out, see if there are any questions, and move on. Perhaps, after you speak your piece, you may even go above and beyond and ask questions like: Does that make sense? Do you understand? Was that clear? Such questions are well-intended but ultimately useless. (I'm just as guilty of using them myself from time to time.)

They tell you if you've been understood. But the problem isn't *if* you've been understood, it's *how* the other person has understood you.

In the paper-ripping exercise, I often ask the rippers to nod if they understand every instruction. They *always* nod. Understanding took place, but I can never predict exactly how they'll interpret my words. How could I? Only they know their interpretation and I never ask them how they've interpreted my instructions. I only tell them what I want them to do.

The two types of miscommunication

Let's make that paper-ripping illustration crystal clear: turn one of those folded, torn pieces of paper into the visible representation of the last miscommunication that cost you at the office. Then imagine all of the other very different pages as the miscommunications of your coworkers and managers. Envision just how many ideas, projects, and, yes, even relationships, are consequently wadded up and thrown away because their outcome didn't match the requestor's intent. With such a visual, it's easy to see how you're losing a day of work every week simply due to miscommunications. So how can you fix the problem and get back that lost day?

First, let's discuss the two major types of miscommunications.

- **VISIBLE MISCOMMUNICATIONS** occur when you speak and can immediately tell you're not being understood. The other person looks at you funny or replies to your email with a confused emoji. So, in the moment, you reword your message and try again. It's easy to spot and solve this kind of miscommunication with minimal time and effort. They aren't costly. Let's move on to the kind of miscommunications that are.

- **INVISIBLE MISCOMMUNICATIONS** occur when you don't know they're occurring. They happen when you've been understood but misinterpreted. We discuss what we need to do, then split up to go work on it for a day, week, or month, only realizing something is wrong when we later get back together. These are the miscommunications that cost us because you only discover them *after* you've wasted time and effort going in the wrong direction. They are the key drivers behind our lost 7.47 hours per week.

My blunder with The Boss is one example of invisible miscommunication, but here's an example likely closer to home. When someone tells you, "I'll get that to you by end of day," what are they saying? Is that 5 p.m. or midnight? The end of your day or the end of theirs? Can it wait until they start work the next morning? We all know what "end of day" means—understanding takes place—but our interpretations can vary widely. More often than not, misunderstanding what someone else means by "end of day" won't ruin a career. But it could. Just imagine how big of an impact even a small misalignment like this can have when it happens again and again as you're defining a months-long project, or even just talking about what you need to get done this week.

Solving for invisible miscommunications in the moment, before the wasted work and effort, is where you can get back hours every week.

Visible Miscommunications	**Invisible Miscommunications**
• Clear signal back that you have not been understood	• Understanding is there, but you don't know how your words have been interpreted
• Obvious in the moment	• Tough to spot in the moment
• Quick to correct	• Costly (time, effort, emotion) to correct

The solution to invisible miscommunications

To stop invisible miscommunications, you have to find a way to make them visible. You want to make them obvious in advance so you can fix them before paying the price of doing the wrong work. You already have the tools to solve visible miscommunications. How can you apply those to eliminating an invisible problem? The following proven communication tactic is so simple you're going to wonder why everyone isn't already using it.

But first, a quiz: What do a soldier, doctor, and pilot all have in common?

If you guessed anything along the lines of critical communication, you win. All three of these professions pay the highest price for their miscommunications: death. When a doctor, soldier, or pilot miscommunicates, they could easily endanger the lives of others.

Landing on the wrong runway, giving a patient the wrong medication, or sending soldiers to the wrong location can have catastrophic consequences. These kinds of miscommunications simply cannot happen in these professions. Out of life-or-death necessity, each of these professions has come up with their own variation of a single technique to eliminate invisible miscommunications.

The brief back asks a listener to repeat back what they heard in their own words. This immediately reveals whether an invisible miscommunication has taken place. You will unquestionably know how the other person interpreted your meaning because they'll have just told you.

MAKE INVISIBLE MISCOMMUNICATIONS VISIBLE WITH A **BRIEF BACK, A REPETITION** OF THE INITIAL MESSAGE IN THE LISTENER'S OWN WORDS.

A common misconception about communication is that great communication ends when the words leave our mouths (or inboxes, keyboards, etc.). This is wrong. To ensure communication has been clear, you also need to know *how* someone has heard and interpreted your message.

This is why questions like "Does that make sense?" don't help. Such questions tell you that you've been understood in general, but not if you've been understood the way you wanted to be. In actuality, you can only be sure that clear communication has occurred when you hear your intention repeated back to you in the other person's own words. This gives you the opportunity to correct any gaps that might exist. For example:

> You: "Jason, please have your TPS report done by end of day."

> Me: "No problem. I'll get that to you then."

> You: "Wait, could you tell me what you mean by end of day?"

> Me: "Sure. I'll get it to you before I head to bed tonight."

> You: "Oh, actually, by end of day I meant 5 p.m. Is that possible?"

Miscommunication avoided.

Just imagine how the game of Broken Telephone would go if kids used brief backs. Before whispering the message they think they heard to the next kid in line, they employ brief backs and first whisper it back to the person who told it to them to be sure they got it right. That game would be boring and unfunny, but it would be an effective way to teach kids how to avoid miscommunications when it really matters.

Not using the brief back is the mistake I made with our *Night At* negotiations. I assumed my words were clear and even asked if I was understood, but I never asked someone to repeat back *how* they'd understood my words. If I had, I would have immediately seen a critical disconnect. If I'd made the invisible miscommunication visible, I could have corrected the problem in the moment.

How to effectively use the brief back

Once I learned about brief backs, the question wasn't if they had a place in office settings, but rather how I could routinely put them to work. Used well, the brief back has the potential to completely eliminate all invisible miscommunications before they have a chance to start. Obviously, most office settings are very different from the life-or-death situations faced by soldiers, doctors, and pilots. What we need is a way to make brief backs work outside of those mission-critical environments.

To figure this out, I experimented. I tried asking my team for brief backs in all sorts of different ways. I learned that there are a lot of ways to get it wrong and a much smaller number of ways to get it right. There are basically two approaches to deploying brief backs: the safe way and the asshole way. Consider these two examples:

1. "Tell me what I just told you. I want to make sure you were listening."
2. "Can you let me know what you took away from this conversation so I can be sure I did a good job getting my point across?"

Guess which one works better?

When I coach folks on using the brief back, the number one concern I hear is, "But I'll sound like an asshole asking for a repetition back." This is a real risk (and I say that from experience).

Option 1 puts you squarely in that territory. It's condescending, passive-aggressive, and rude. I don't recommend asking for brief backs this way. From much trial and error, I learned that the key when asking for a brief back is to focus on yourself, not on the other person. The brief back should confirm that *you* did a good job of communicating, not that the other person did a good job listening. The idea is that if something went wrong then it's on you, not them.

Notice the focus of Option 2: "*I* can be sure *I* did a good job." This clearly signals to the other person that you're looking for feedback on the job *you* did and not checking on something they did or didn't do. Following this general approach, I've rarely if ever seen anyone have an issue with being asked for a brief back.

WHEN ASKING FOR A BRIEF BACK, **FOCUS ON YOURSELF, NOT ON THE OTHER PERSON.**

As a disclaimer, brief backs are awkward and scary to use at first. To help, I recommend starting to deploy them when you're the listener, i.e., deliver the brief back instead of asking for it at first. For some reason, this tends to feel easier. Once you're comfortable briefing others back when they tell you something, then you can graduate to asking for brief backs as the speaker. Here's how to use the brief back when you're listening to others:

"I think what you just told me is [insert the message you heard]. Did I get that right?"

This is a great way to confirm that your interpretation of what you were told matches the other person's intent. Again, notice the approach of keeping it focused on yourself. Rather than telling someone you want to make sure they communicated well, you're asking if *you* understood correctly. Keeping the focus on yourself makes the other person feel comfortable and keeps the brief back in a safe and supportive space.

These methods work great when you're talking to someone face-to-face, over the phone, or on a video call. They work much less well for written communication like instant messaging and email, since you'd effectively be asking someone to copy and paste your words back to you. As more and more offices shift to hybrid or remote structures, it's even more important than ever to brief each other back. In asynchronous settings, I recommend briefing back with something like:

"Can you let me know what you plan to do next so I can best support you?"

Hearing what someone is going to do with what you've just told them is a great way to make sure you're aligned.

When to use brief backs

Brief backs are powerful, but you probably won't want to use them all the time.

> You: "Hey, Jason, want to grab lunch?"
>
> Me: "Sure. What do you feel like?"
>
> You: "I'm craving Thai food."
>
> Me: "I think what you just told me is that you want Thai for lunch. Is that right?"
>
> You: "Umm, yes. Are you feeling OK, Jason?"

Other than the obvious issues with a never-ending loop of me briefing back your brief back of my brief back, not all situations need one. So the question is: When should you use a brief back?

Most people I work with start using the brief back based on their perceived likelihood of a miscommunication happening. For example, maybe you're talking to a person on your team whom you work with every day. You think it's unlikely they'll misunderstand you, so you don't ask for a brief back. I don't recommend this approach. In my experience, our ability to predict an invisible miscommunication is low, hence the invisibility of the problem in the first place.

Instead, use brief backs based on the cost of the possible miscommunication. Set a threshold for yourself. Everyone's threshold is a bit different. Use a brief back for anything above that threshold... like if, perhaps, a multifaceted, multi-organization, big budget event hinges on it. For anything below your threshold, like what you'll have for lunch, you can skip the brief back so your colleagues won't assume you're already mentally out to lunch.

I use brief backs in any situation where I feel like the cost will be high, even if I think the probability of a miscommunication happening is very low. Brief backs are quick—a few seconds for me to ask for it and a few more for you to give it—so the cost of using one when you don't need it is minimal. On the other hand, the cost of needing a brief back and not using it is high. Think about your tolerance for wasted time and use a brief back whenever you think a miscommunication would exceed that. "Better safe than sorry" is a good guiding principle here.

You're not the boss of me

Ultimately, the *Night At* happened. No, Springsteen did not move his concert (Boss move to the end). Luckily for me, the incredible team I was working with found a way to juggle the stadium's schedule and open up back-to-back hockey and basketball games. The event was saved and turned out to be one of the most successful initiatives I've ever been a part of. But it came at the expense of a *significant* amount of extra work, effort, and stress that could have been avoided had I just asked a six-second question: "Can you let me know what you took away from this conversation so I can be sure I did a good job getting my point across?"

Note to self: When you royally mess up, learn from the failure.

ACTION EXERCISE

Over the next two weeks, try brief backs.

- **Week 1:** Give people brief backs *after* they share something with you. This is the easiest way to start and will get you and others around you comfortable with the concept of brief backs.

- **Week 2:** Start asking people for brief backs when you share something with them. Remember: keep it about you, not them.

Further reading in case you feel like it

- *Never Split the Difference*, Chris Voss and Tahl Raz—This is my favorite book on negotiations. The reason why I included it here is because it's really about listening, and there's a lot to learn from this book beyond how to negotiate.

- *Crucial Conversations*, Joseph Grenny, Kerry Patterson, Ron McMillan, Al Switzler, and Emily Gregory—Although this book is geared more toward emotionally charged communications, it provides a great foundation for communicating effectively in any situation.

- *Extreme Ownership*, Jocko Willink and Leif Babin—There's something about the way leadership is described in this book that strikes a chord for me. You should read this book if you're interested in reframing how you think about your role in any given situation.

TOO MANY COOKS IN THE KITCHEN

How to Speed Up Slow Decision-Making

There are basically no companies that have good slow decisions.
There are only companies that have good fast decisions.

—LARRY PAGE

How many times have you felt frustrated with slow decision-making at work? You know what you need to do, but you're stuck waiting around for someone else to make a decision so you can move forward. Or you get called into a meeting to discuss a topic that should have been decided days, if not weeks, ago.

It feels like the more people involved in a decision, the more it seems to slowly grind to a halt. A team of two can take twice as long to make a decision you'd make on your own in half the time. A team of ten or more? That can circle endlessly. But do more people always mean you'll move more slowly? Let's play a game...

How long do you think it would take a team of about 400,000 people with a budget totaling over $250 billion to make a decision? That's a big team. They must move slowly. What if I also told you that their decisions are incredibly risky, that a bad decision could kill someone, and that they cannot use chat, email, or cell phones to help them communicate while making decisions? Even more slowdowns, right?

This isn't a hypothetical situation. I'm describing a real team that worked on a project you've heard of at a company you know. Take a moment and try to guess how long they took to make decisions. (Bonus points if you can name the company as well.) Even if you smell a trick and assume they move faster than you'd expect, I'll bet the answer will still surprise you.

Too many cooks in the kitchen

A while back I was helping Andrew, the chief operating officer at a company I work with, prepare for an upcoming meeting where his team had to make an important decision. He and others had done prework to outline their options, share relevant information, and bring everyone else involved up to speed. Walking into the two-hour session, he felt confident they had what they needed to reach a decision. When I caught up with him about a week later, he told me the meeting was great. The debate was both fiery and respectful. Everyone left feeling energized about how much ground they'd covered. This sounded promising until I asked him what decision they made. You might not have an answer yet for that 400,000-person team, but I'll bet you can guess what decision Andrew's team made.

Yup, nothing. Well, not quite nothing. They did decide when to meet next to talk about the decision some more. This went on for a few weeks. They felt like they were making progress in the moment, but looking back, it was clear they were in an endless cycle of debate and discussion. I eventually asked Andrew what was happening and why the breakdown occurred. He told me, "Too many cooks in the kitchen."

We've all been there. Sitting through meeting after meeting where the only decision that gets made is when to meet again to discuss the decision even more. Your team needs a decision that has implications for other teams and, as more people weigh in, progress seems to stop.

It doesn't have to be this way.

Escape velocity

How long did it take that team of 400,000 people with a budget totaling over $250 billion to make a decision?

One single day.

That's a very big team making very fast decisions. No more waiting around to get started on a good idea. No more meetings to decide on more meetings. Think about your team today. When was the last time you made a meaningful decision in a single day?

In the 1960s, NASA's $250 billion Apollo moon landing project employed around 400,000 people and they regularly made highly complicated, very risky decisions in a single day. In one of the most ambitious projects ever undertaken by humans, NASA needed only seven years to go from the first American in space to landing humans on the moon. Almost as amazing as the moon landing itself was the teamwork and decision-making that made it happen. There's a lot to learn from how NASA worked together.

So that the incredibly large organization could move faster without sacrificing quality, NASA brought in George Mueller in 1963. He quickly reset operations by focusing on decision-making and overhauled how teams worked together. Asked how they were able to land on the moon in seven short years, an employee later said this about their decision-making: "It got to a point where we could identify a problem in the morning and by the close of business we could solve it, get the money allocated, get the decisions made and get things working."

In my work helping teams speed up their decision-making, I often hear pushback like:

- "Our decisions are complicated."
- "We need a lot of people to weigh in."
- "It's a high-risk decision that we need to be careful with."

That's when I share the NASA story.

- Are your decisions more complicated than sending humans 768,800 kilometers to the moon and back on a rocket with over 3 million parts?
- Are more than 400,000 people involved?
- Are the risks higher than keeping people alive with a computer less than 1.5 percent as capable as the phone in your pocket?

The point quickly becomes clear. Too many cooks in the kitchen isn't the problem—unless you count that time in 1965 when John Young disagreed with NASA's actual cooks and secretly smuggled a corned beef sandwich into orbit, sparking a public safety hearing on the dangers of sandwich crumbs in space (corned beef wouldn't fly again until 1981).

You may not need to move as fast as 1960's NASA, but your team can definitely make decisions faster than they do today. NASA proved that decisions don't need to slow down as you add more people.

Teams can make good decisions quickly—even big teams. With three specific tactics, I'll share how you can help your team get to decisions in a fraction of the time it usually takes. You'll avoid meetings that only make more meetings. Decisions will happen faster, feel far less frustrating, and save you and your team from *hours* of unproductive work every week.

Sound like a moon shot?

The cost of slow decision-making

The data on how we use our time on decision-making is conclusive: we are wasting huge amounts of it. In surveying 1,200 managers across a range of companies, McKinsey & Co. discovered that managers spend an estimated 37 percent of their time on decision-making. These managers also self-reported that over *half* of this time is wasted. Assuming a standard forty-hour workweek, that's more than one full day per week of useless decision-making activities. That's staggering. It's comparable to a decision that should be made in two weeks taking over a month.

Hours Spent on Decision-Making per Week

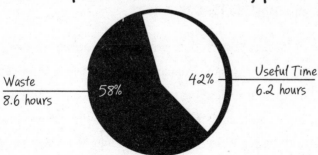

Waste
8.6 hours

58%

42%

Useful Time
6.2 hours

If you report to a manager, you might be thinking: *I knew my manager wasn't great at decision-making. They have a big problem to fix in wasting all that time!* Hold that thought. Who do you think is wasting all of this time with them? (Well, not *you*, of course, but certainly the other people you work with.)

SPEEDING UP SLOW DECISION-MAKING WILL **SAVE YOU UP TO A DAY EVERY WEEK.**

We're all wasting time due to slow decision-making. The good news is that you have an opportunity to reclaim up to a full day every single week without any change to your impact if you can learn to make decisions more efficiently. One full day less effort with no reduction in your output. Think of what you could do with that.

So why is slow decision-making such a professional epidemic?

Our brains are wired for consensus

For most of human history, our evolution has depended on being part of a larger social group. We simply wouldn't have survived on our own. As a result, belonging to a group is such a deeply seated need that some psychologists have argued it's more important to us than food and shelter. Research has even shown that being excluded from a group activates the same regions of our brains as physical pain. As a result, upsetting the balance in social situations, like disagreeing with your team at work, isn't easy. You probably don't have to think that hard to remember a time when you disagreed and kept it to yourself. As humans we want to agree with one another—and potentially even need to—because we care so deeply about getting along.

Our brains are wired for consensus. Yet we're actively building teams that create more controversy. This formula illustrates how disagreement grows on teams:

MORE PEOPLE + MORE DIVERSITY = MORE DISAGREEMENT

As we add more people to our teams and they bring a greater diversity of thought, we are actually creating the conditions for more disagreement. Research findings are crystal clear that teams are better in pretty much every way when they're made up of diverse thinkers. We need diversity, but with diversity necessarily comes differences of opinion. Left unaddressed, this is what slows down decision-making. Instead of embracing disagreements and making decisions anyway, our bias for agreement pushes us toward time-consuming compromises and consensus-building we don't need.

Disagreement is the superpower of diversity. It can make all of your decisions better, but diversity can also significantly slow them down. So, the question is: How do you adapt your decision-making approach to leverage the superpower of diversity without the slowdown of always having to agree?

For faster decisions, learn to disagree better

Though it might feel somewhat paradoxical, better disagreement leads to faster decisions. Think about the last time your team all agreed on a decision. You probably didn't waste any time talking about what decision to make. You just made it and got back to work. When everyone agrees, decisions aren't all that hard.

But momentum dies when one, two, or ten people disagree. Each person becomes more focused on reaching an *agreement* than on making the decision itself. The cycle of debates, discussions, and endless meetings continues. The decision is tabled, another meeting is scheduled, and another hour of your future workweek is lost. Finding a compromise or complete consensus might make you or your team feel better, but it's rarely needed and often leads to frustrating slowdowns.

Here's the secret: your team can be in alignment without being in agreement.

Once you and your team realize that the goal of a decision is *not* total agreement, you'll move faster. Recognizing that you don't all need to agree enables you to decide sooner, and embracing your disagreements—rather than trying to get rid of them—keeps the quality of your decisions high even as you speed them up. Faster decision-making happens not in spite of disagreements, but *because* of them.

THE BETTER YOU DISAGREE, THE **FASTER YOU'LL DECIDE.**

This chapter is not about how to better argue your ideas, find compromises, or get everyone to agree with you. Instead, it's about how the following three essential tactics can help you productively disagree so you can make decisions faster as a team:

1. Decide who decides.
2. Collect context, not opinions.
3. Seek alignment, not agreement.

Following each of these tactics will teach you how to save a full day of wasted work every single week.

Decide who decides

You and your team can't make a decision until you know who is going to decide. Agree or disagree, decisions don't just happen on their own. Somebody has to make them. I can't tell you how often this simple first step in decision-making is completely missed. How often have you been deep in debate without clarity on who the decision-maker is?

This is what was happening to Andrew's team. After weeks of meetings without any decision, he took a step back. Before diving into the discussion at their next meeting, Andrew asked, "Who is making this decision?" When two hands shot up, he thought, *I just made this worse.* However, what happened next shows the power of this simple but crucial step.

47

The team shifted their debate from the decision itself to deciding who would decide. Once they knew exactly how they were going to close the debate by identifying the decision-maker, they went back to their initial discussion. By the end of that meeting, the designated decision-maker had everything they needed and *made a decision*. Andrew told me, "It was unbelievable. We didn't all agree, but we all aligned behind the decision and got moving on doing the actual work. Once we got clear on who was going to decide, our progress skyrocketed."

BEFORE YOU DEBATE ANY DECISION, **DECIDE WHO WILL DECIDE.**

If you take nothing else away from this chapter, let it be this: always stop and ask, "Who is making this decision?" before diving into the decision itself. This single tactic alone will save you hours of wasted effort. You'll be surprised how often the actual decision-maker isn't clear and how much faster you'll move once your team has that clarity.

Why does this work so effectively? We get stuck in endless debates, discussions, and analyses because we don't know how we are ultimately going to decide. This is especially important when we don't all agree. A clear decision-maker can decide in the presence of disagreement. Without one, teams default to compromise and consensus because there's no defined way to break ties.

Other than deciding by consensus—which I would not recommend for the vast majority of situations—there are essentially two ways of making decisions on any team:

Who Decides?	How Disagreements Are Handled
A specific person	That person will decide considering all context available, including any disagreements.
A vote	A vote, like majority rules, ultimately decides for the group. Any disagreements that may have existed are put aside following the vote.

When a clear decision-maker is assigned, you're inherently choosing how you'll know when enough is enough and you're ready to decide. Rather than waiting for consensus—which may never happen—you now have an agreed-upon way to make a final choice. If you do choose to go the route of consensus, at least do so on purpose. That way, you don't waste time trying to get everyone to agree when you don't need to (which should be most of the time).

Often, you'll ask who is deciding and no one will know. This can be another big waste of time, so here are three suggestions to help you decide who is best to decide:

- **Choose the person who works closest to the context of the decision day-to-day.** For example, if you're deciding what copy to use in a marketing campaign, the decision should probably be made by the person who works most often on that marketing project, not their manager.

- **Choose yourself.** Ask your manager, "What would need to be true for me to make this decision?" The more decisions you make, the better you'll get at making them. If your manager says no, showing this initiative will likely result in them keeping you in mind for future decisions.

- **If you're a manager, choose to delegate.** Most decisions don't need you to decide unless they are truly mission-critical and very hard to change later. By delegating, you take a task off your plate while also creating growth opportunities for others.

Once you know who the decision-maker is, set a date for when they need to decide. This holds them accountable, and research has shown that implementation intentions (i.e., setting a date) significantly increases the likelihood they'll get it done on time. To speed up your process even further, ask, "What would need to be true to make this decision sooner?" The language here is important. You're not asking a yes-or-no question like, "Can we make this decision sooner?" Rather, you're seeking specifics on what would have to be true to make the decision faster. You'll be surprised how this question can open up creative ideas to increase pace.

Share context, not opinions

When NASA was building rockets to send people to the moon, they needed fast decisions, but they also needed good decisions. Moving quickly doesn't matter if you're making big mistakes, a lesson NASA and the rest of the world learned all too well nearly twenty years after the moon landing missions. Over time, NASA had slowly forgotten its own lessons, slipping back into a slow-moving bureaucracy. They paid the ultimate price for it. At 11:39 a.m. Eastern Standard Time on January 28, 1986, a failed O-ring caused the explosion of the *Challenger* space shuttle just seventy-three seconds into its flight, tragically killing all seven crew members.

The temperature on launch day was a brisk 2°C (36°F), which was 10°C (17°F) below the O-ring's minimum safe operating temperature. This issue was raised as a clear launch-aborting situation to key decision-makers, but they decided to go ahead anyway. A comprehensive retroactive study later found that the mechanical failure of the O-ring caused a fuel leak leading to the explosion, and that the decision-making failure now commonly known as *groupthink* caused the terrible decision to launch in the first place.

Groupthink refers to the challenges we face making decisions in group settings. It's different from peer pressure, where we consciously decide to go with the flow, even if we know it isn't the best idea. Unlike peer pressure, we have no idea that groupthink is happening to us. Behind the scenes, our brains shift from deciding based on a rational analysis of the facts to making decisions based on popularity. We unknowingly overweight other people's opinions because of our subconscious desire to fit in. A few knew *Challenger* had to abort. A great many more wanted the mission to go ahead. Rationality was no match for millions of years of evolution.

To make good decisions at pace, your goal is to collect the diverse context of what everyone is thinking while reducing the probability of bad decisions from groupthink. Since it's subconscious, you can't entirely stop groupthink from happening. You can, however, rethink what you and others say to reduce the likelihood that it occurs.

The best approach is counterintuitive: stop telling people what you would do. Don't tell them what decision you think they should make. Instead, tell them what you know so they can make the best decision possible. Describe the context you would consider as part of making the decision, but don't tell them your opinion about what you would decide. This helps to avoid groupthink because, instead of sharing a biasing opinion, you're sharing richer, more diverse thinking to help the decision-maker make their own choice. If they never hear your opinion, they can't be biased by it.

DON'T TELL PEOPLE WHAT YOU WOULD DO. INSTEAD, **TELL THEM WHAT YOU KNOW.**

Keeping opinions to yourself is a lot harder than it sounds. Our natural inclination is to help others by sharing what we think they should do. Your friends and colleagues probably tell you all the time what they would do if they were you. When they do, they're biasing you, even if you don't realize it. You don't need more opinions.

Instead of telling the decision-maker what you would decide, tell them what you know that they don't. Since you can't know what they don't know, I find it's best to overshare. Tell them all of the factors you think are important and all of the information you think is relevant. (We'll cover how to do this more in Chapter 7, "How to Make Better Decisions"). If you're the decision-maker, tell people the context you're considering and ask them, "What am I missing?" This will help your team focus on filling in your blind spots rather than telling you what they would do.

Sharing context instead of opinions doesn't just improve decisions, it also helps speed them up. Opinions are essentially endless. For every person you ask, you'll get another opinion. Information, on the other hand, is limited. There is only so much your team can realistically know before making a decision. After working on a decision for a while, you'll notice that although more opinions may continue to come up, new information will plateau. Once you stop hearing new information, it's a sign that you (or whoever is deciding) have what you need to make a decision. When you stop hearing new context, start deciding.

Decisions on your team can only get better when everyone's thinking is out in the open. That means you have to find a way to get your voice heard. A classic extrovert might hear an idea and right then and there stand up in front of all of their colleagues to share what they think. An introvert, on the other hand, might need to go home, sleep, take a shower, and collect their thoughts before sharing them in an email. There's no right or wrong way to add your thinking to the mix, so long as you find some way. Sharing what you know, not what decision you would make, is how you keep decision quality high even at pace.

Seek alignment, not agreement
Good teams are diverse teams. Diverse teams disagree. We've covered how to make decisions faster by setting a clear decision-maker and how to maintain quality even as you decide more quickly

by sharing context, not opinions. The question now is: How do you move past disagreements when they occur? If you want to productively disagree, your team should focus on alignment, not agreement.

Great teams can both disagree and commit. Read that again.

Great teams can recognize genuine disagreements and decide to move forward together anyway. The idea is to share your thinking and argue vehemently, but once a decision is made, support it as if it were your own. If you have a deep ethical disagreement, by all means stand your ground. In all other situations, it's better to commit once a decision has been made. The key is to recognize when the moment for debate has passed. Once the necessary context has been shared and a decision has been made, it's time to support it, not debate it further.

Signs of Productive Disagreement	Signs of Unproductive Disagreement
• The decision-maker is clear.	• We continue to argue our opinions even after we've shared all the context we have.
• Everyone involved feels heard and knows they contributed.	• We say we're committed, but really we're waiting to say, "I told you so" when things don't work out.
• The decision is understood and the team is aligned on why the chosen option was selected.	• We don't talk about the decision as if it were our own, deferring potential future blame to the decision-maker.

This tactic may be the most difficult because it requires you to hold two competing points of view in mind at the same time: that you disagree with a decision and *fully* support it. Your job when you disagree and commit is to stop trying to get everyone to agree, and instead start figuring out what to do next, as if the disagreement never existed in the first place.

DISAGREEING AND COMMITTING MEANS SUPPORTING A DECISION YOU DON'T AGREE WITH **AS IF IT WERE YOUR OWN DECISION.**

You've probably already felt the benefits of someone else's ability to disagree and commit. If you've ever had a job interview and were subsequently hired, someone found at least one reason *not* to hire you. I'm sorry to break that to you—I'm sure they were wrong. But the decision-maker, looking across all of your strengths and weaknesses, ultimately said, "Yes, this is the person we need." At that point, the team committed to you as the new hire, even though there was at least one reason not to. If that one naysayer hadn't committed, they wouldn't be fully supportive of you in your new role. They'd have set you up for failure before you even started.

Great teams can both disagree and commit. I know this tactic can be challenging, so here's how I commit to a decision that I don't agree with.

How to disagree and commit

First, I need to know that any context I had was both heard and considered. Being heard doesn't mean that I'll get what I want. It means I know my thinking was considered as part of the decision-making process. The best way to help people feel heard is to use a written framework (more on how to do that in Chapter 7, "How to Make Better Decisions") so everyone involved can see what went into making a decision.

Second, when I'm wrestling with committing to a decision I don't agree with, I ask myself, "What would need to be true for me to fully support this decision even though I can't agree?" I use this very specific language intentionally.

- "What would need to be true...?" pushes me to list how I can support the decision rather than getting fixated on whether or not I agree.
- "...even though I can't agree" helps me recognize that we're at the point where an agreement isn't going to happen, and any further debate isn't helpful.

ASK YOURSELF, "WHAT WOULD NEED TO BE TRUE FOR ME TO **FULLY SUPPORT THIS DECISION EVEN THOUGH I CAN'T AGREE?"**

A note on second-guessing

When I talk to teams about disagreeing and committing, they'll often ask whether past decisions should be challenged. When you revisit a decision without any new information, all you're doing is second-guessing yourself. That's a distraction and a colossal waste of time. Don't reopen a decision if there isn't any new information. You already considered what there was to consider. However, when new and relevant information comes up that makes you think differently about a past decision, definitely bring it up. Just make sure you come prepared with a clear callout of the new information you didn't have the first time around. A big benefit of making decisions more quickly is that you get to act sooner and learn from whatever happens. Don't let second-guessing distract you. Focus on moving forward and learning as you go.

One small step

In an obscure 1998 interview, George Mueller talked about his time leading the moon landing missions. There's one moment in the interview you have to be watching for or you'll miss it. Mueller is asked how he felt the moment they landed on the moon: "It was sort of anti-climactic."

That is a direct quote. Possibly the single greatest technological achievement in history and the person in charge, who was often referred to as one of NASA's most brilliant managers, was expecting more? He was so focused on the details and decisions required to make it all happen that the moon landing itself paled in comparison. If faster decision-making can eclipse an event like that, it's bound to have an impact for you and your team too.

Thanks to NASA's hard work, we know decisions don't need to slow down as more people get involved. We know we're going to disagree more as we build diverse teams. We also know that it's what we do with these disagreements that determines whether they make us better or burn us out with needlessly slow decision-making.

Striving for compromises and trying to get everyone to agree is unnecessarily costing you and your team up to a day every single week. The better your team disagrees, the faster (and better) it will decide.

You can do this by:

1. Asking "Who is deciding?" before debating the decision itself.
2. Sharing context, not opinions, in order to avoid groupthink.
3. Seeking alignment, not agreement, to move forward even when you can't agree.

If you take only one small step, ask: "Who is deciding?"

It'll give you and your team one giant leap.

ACTION EXERCISE

For every decision you're a part of over the next two weeks, ask: "Who is making this decision?"

At the end of your two weeks, reflect on the experience:

- How often was the decision-maker clear to everyone?
- Did the pace speed up or slow down once the decision-maker was clear?
- Did the decision-maker make a decision?

Further reading in case you feel like it

- *Team of Teams*, General Stanley McChrystal, Tantum Collins, David Silverman, and Chris Fussell—This is a great book on the dynamics of teamwork and how to find ways to work more fluidly together. It's a bit process and structure heavy, but there's good wisdom in here if you can work through it.

- *Principles*, Ray Dalio—I hesitated to add this because it is a big book with a lot of detail you may not need. I wound up putting it in because it's such a comprehensive deep dive into many decision-making tactics that you're sure to find a few solid nuggets.

- *Atomic Habits*, James Clear—There's a reason this book has sold a copy roughly every fifteen seconds since it was published. Lots in here about how to build new habits and keep them going, both at work and outside of it.

NEVER TRUST
A CHEAP
LUNCH

How to Take Back
Control of Your Time

Perfection is achieved, not when there is nothing more to add, but when there is nothing left to take away.

—ANTOINE DE SAINT-EXUPÉRY

Where to go for lunch is always a hot topic at any office. Years ago, I worked for an early-stage artificial intelligence company and a teammate made a questionable choice about where to eat that always stuck with me. I met Katharine when she joined the company as our first intern. She advanced quickly, becoming an incredibly strong operator, and regularly shared creative ideas for complicated, cross-functional challenges. Over the years we worked together, I learned to trust her instincts when it came to tough decisions. One day, however, she walked into the office excited about a lunch special that sounded like a less-than-stellar idea: $1.00 for a full week of lunches.

Yes, you read that correctly. Not a dollar a day. One dollar for the whole week. Sounds too good to be true? Not to Katharine.

I'm sure you can guess what happened next.

She made it through an impressive four days before getting sick. Not so sick that she stopped coming into work, but sick enough that she later told me all she could eat was dry toast and she was fast asleep by 7 p.m. every night. Eventually—and much longer than I would have held out—she saw a doctor. Diagnosis: salmonella poisoning.

At twenty cents a meal, it's not all that surprising she got sick. What is surprising, however, is that she kept coming into work. Katharine is incredibly smart, but she had somehow convinced herself every day *for a month* that other people's requests at work were more important than her own health. This is an extreme example, but before you judge her, think about how often you take on things you know you shouldn't.

How often in your life and at work do you put other people's requests above your own? How long does it take before your week gets away from you and you have no time left for what *you* need to get done? It doesn't feel great to work hard all week and yet still feel like you have an endless to-do list at the end of it.

Steve Jobs put it well: "People think focus means saying yes to the thing you've got to focus on. But that's not what it means at all. It means saying no to the hundred other good ideas that there are."

I think we all know we need to say no more, but it's really hard. No one ever explains how to do it well. Forget Katharine's iron stomach (and will) for a moment, and what you're left with is a common desire you probably share to do a good job and help your team as much as possible. You want to say yes, so you regularly take on all sorts of new requests on top of an already full week.

What if you could learn to say no more effectively, with less guilt and less fear of judgment from others? What if you could spend more time on your most important priorities for the week and actually get them done? What if your time really was *your* time?

Anyone can achieve this, from the intern to the CEO. In the previous two chapters, we discussed how to save a full day of work every week by avoiding time-consuming miscommunications and speeding up slow decision-making on your team. But even if you accomplish those goals, you won't feel their benefits without a better ability to say no. Even if you shave a few hours out of your week, you'll likely fill them right back up again without noticing. Whether or not those hours are meaningfully filled is up to you. That's why learning to say no is the crucial final step in accomplishing five days of work in four and unblocking a better week.

Why you don't say no as often as you should

Remember groupthink from the previous chapter, that quirk in our brains that unknowingly shifts rational decision-making toward conforming with other people's opinions? It turns out that another subconscious shift impacts your ability to plan. You, me, and anyone else with a human brain pretty much sucks at estimating how long a task will take. Psychologists call it the planning fallacy, and it effectively means we expect to get way more done than we actually can. How often do you get through a day or a week with a completely finished to-do list?

Thanks to the planning fallacy, most of us take on too much, setting ourselves up for failure and over allocating our time before a week has even begun. Then you get into the office and your boss asks you to put together a report you hadn't expected. No sooner do you get to work on it than your colleague comes over with "Just a quick question." Twenty-seven minutes into answering that "quick" question, an all-team message dings, alerting everyone to meet in the conference room ASAP. That meeting drags just enough into your lunch hour that you're mildly angry—even the discount lunch begins to seem appealing. By the time you've eaten and sat back down at your desk, the day is more than halfway done and you've yet to check a single box on your own to-do list.

This story is facetious, of course, but it's not far from reality. The fact is that a majority of us *don't want to say no to others*. We want to be seen as helpful, courteous, and professional. But again, at what expense? If we could all learn to say no in the right way to the right things at the right time, wouldn't we all be more productive and happier in our jobs?

It's not your fault that you don't say no enough. As humans evolved to live in communities, we developed to value helping one another and keeping track of who was helping whom. Helping became part of surviving. No one had space in their tribe for freeloaders. That's one reason, as a species, we feel so guilty just thinking about saying no to someone else. *What will they think of me? Will they help me later when I need them?*

When you don't say no enough, you take on more than you can ever get done. Your own priorities at work suffer, or you cut into family, sleep, or personal time to make up the difference. It's not until you're significantly overloaded that the pain of saying no feels better than the pain of taking on more. Research has shown that you'll wait until you've built up a full day of additional work on top of your already full week before you finally break down and say no because you're overwhelmed. By this point, it's too late. You're well down the path toward burning out because you didn't say no earlier.

Conventional wisdom tells you to focus on your methodology—to optimize your time better—but the key to better prioritization isn't methodology, it's psychology. It's a mindset shift to focus on *what you won't do* that makes you more effective at what you will do. When you're better able to say no, your time will become your own again. You'll stop overplanning, and you'll avoid the endless distractions that lead to constantly feeling overwhelmed.

BETTER PRIORITIZATION IS ABOUT PSYCHOLOGY, NOT METHODOLOGY.

Not doing is harder than you think

It's incredibly hard to intentionally *not* do something. For instance, *don't* think about a polka-dotted elephant.

How'd that go for you? I bet not so well. You were probably picturing our polka-dotted pachyderm friend the moment you read the words. You can't *not* think about it. And the more I write it, the more you're thinking about it—even though I told you not to. It's easy to think about something and really hard to intentionally not think about it. The same is true at work. Even when you tell yourself not to, you still wind up checking your email in a meeting or letting a "quick" conversation expand into an hour-long, off-topic brainstorm. It's much more difficult to have the discipline *not* to do these things.

Once again, your brain is working against you. It *craves* distraction. Your prefrontal cortex, the part of your brain largely responsible for complex cognitive functions like planning, decision-making, etc. (a.k.a. working), has a novelty bias. You're naturally drawn toward something new, like checking a notification that just came in rather than working on that report you've been focused on for the past hour. Making matters worse, whenever you do jump to something new, your brain releases the feel-good chemical dopamine, further reinforcing your behavior to prioritize distraction.

Research has shown that on average you're losing about two hours every day to distractions at work. That's more than a full day you can claim back every single week if you're better able to say no when you need to. This is why you're overworked and overwhelmed. It's hard enough to see and avoid your own distractions, let alone say no to someone else when they bring you one.

How to say yes to more no

What do traffic lights, Band-Aids, and a can of beer all have in common? They were all invented before the word *priorities*. Until the 1940s, *priority* was singular. You would only have one at any given time. How nice does that sound?

It wasn't until forty years later, in the 1980s, that the word *prioritization* was invented to describe deciding on the relative importance between many different priorities. Since then, we've become obsessed with productivity. We create endless to-do lists and look for new ways to get everything done. But when everything is a priority, nothing is.

Remember Steve Jobs' quote from earlier? Your to-do list doesn't tell you what *not* to do. Shifting your mindset to focus on clearly defining what you won't do is exactly what you need to make more progress on what you will do. When you know what not to do, you're better able to avoid distractions and stay focused on what matters most. It's also easier to take much-needed breaks because you know when you've done enough.

Saying no more often isn't about ignoring everyone and never saying yes again. Rather, saying no well and more often is about building more explicit intent in advance. This upfront and intentional thinking is then used to align—or realign—you with *your* priorities.

Write a not-to-do list

If you plan to take on too much before your week even begins, it's only going to go downhill from there. That's why we're going to take your existing to-do list and complement it with a not-to-do list. The not-to-do list is just what it sounds like: a list of what you're intentionally deciding not to do that week. The right to-do list helps you avoid the pitfalls of the planning fallacy before the week starts, and clarifying your non-priorities in a not-to-do list makes it easier to avoid distractions as the week unfolds.

To set yourself up for a great week, open up your long to-do list and spend fifteen minutes first thing on Monday doing this:

1. Pick your top three most important priorities. *You only get three. I'll share why below.*
2. Put everything else on your not-to-do list. *Yes, everything else.*
3. Only add more to your to-do list if your schedule is wide open after blocking out time for your top three priorities. *Remember the planning fallacy: your top priorities will take longer than you expect.*

What you're aiming for is a short to-do list and a really long not-to-do list of everything else important—yes, important—that you're consciously deciding not to do that week. I've provided a full breakdown of a weekly template and habit you can use at www.yourgrassisgreener.com/resources. A lot of what goes on your not-to-do list is going to feel hard to delay. Even though the idea of a not-to-do list is simple, deciding what to put on it is rarely easy. By definition, it's filled with everything not on your to-do list, so let's start by looking at what you should prioritize and work back from there.

Three big bets

You already know that the planning fallacy has you over allocating your weeks before they begin, so you need to aim for less. I'm sure you've heard the expression *Less is more*. I'm also sure you don't believe in it. When was the last time you got promoted for doing less than everyone else around you or felt amazing about your day because of how little you got done? The idea is right, but it's missing two crucial words to enable you to put it to work: Less *priorities* is more *progress*. If you want to get more done, focus your energy on fewer things. This doesn't mean less impact, just fewer to-dos.

LESS **PRIORITIES** IS MORE **PROGRESS.**

Think of your top priorities as the big bets you're making with your time each week. You're still going to do other smaller tasks, like answering email and attending meetings. What you're trying to capture with your top three priorities are the biggest, most important impact drivers for the week.

Research has shown that our brains are limited to keeping only about three to five main concepts in working memory at any time. It's a lot easier to avoid distractions in the moment if you don't have to think too hard about what your top priorities are. If you feel like experimenting with a lot of up-and-down weeks like I did, you'll see that you can regularly accomplish more than two big bets and that planning for four or five opens up over allocation and overwhelm. Hence the sweet spot of three top priorities per week.

Yes, it's fewer initiatives to really focus on, but you'll move them forward significantly more than if you split your attention across more. If it feels hard to pick only three, that's a sign you're doing something right.

INTENTIONALLY LIMIT YOURSELF TO **THREE BIG BETS** FOR YOUR TIME AND IMPACT EACH WEEK.

How to pick your big bets

To figure out my top three priorities each week, I ask myself:

Even if I accomplish <u>nothing</u> else, this week will still be successful if I...

The more impact an outcome has and the more it unlocks or unblocks other work and people, the more likely it is to become a big bet. Exactly what yours are each week depends on the nature of your job, but some examples include:

- finishing a task so the rest of your team can get to theirs
- delivering a project proposal so your team can decide and move forward
- unblocking a customer or prospect

Keep in mind that it will often feel like you're not planning to get enough done (thanks planning fallacy). Remember, it's much easier to add more work in later than it is to take it out. You're better off planning for less and adding in more if you manage to get it all done than overloading yourself before you've even begun. If you're really struggling with the idea of limiting yourself to three big bets, you can always aim for more progress on each one. Just don't add any more.

Once you're clear on your top priorities for the week, create the space you need to get them done. Move meetings, deprioritize lesser to-dos. Whatever it takes. Since they matter most, you'll want to be sure you start your week with the space you need to make them happen. Only add more to your to-do list if you have space left over after allocating time for your big bets with some buffer just to be safe.

The benefits of your not-to-do list

Your to-do list is done when you've listed your top three priorities. At this point, everything else goes on your not-to-do list. Having so few to-dos and so many not-to-dos will probably make you feel like you're going to underachieve at first—but your results will tell a different story.

Clearly articulating your non-priorities in a not-to-do list helps you keep focused and has a number of bonus benefits as well:

1. **Your mental health will improve.** When you've done what you intended to do, you can feel good about stopping. And you don't have to feel guilty that you're not doing more. You might hit a Friday feeling like you weren't impactful, but a quick review of your week shows that you accomplished your big bets. You can replace those negative thoughts with a feeling of accomplishment.

2. **Your expectation management will improve.** Managing people's expectations is a big part of not letting them down. Once you're clear on what you're not going to do, you can have a chat with anyone who might be affected. (I'll cover how to do this shortly.)

3. **Your organizational skills will improve.** As tasks come up each week and you decide not to do them, add them to your not-to-do list. This will give you a running tally of all the important work you can prioritize in the future. You'll feel more on top of everything because you know it's all captured somewhere.

It's freeing to encounter a new potential priority and respond to it by actively deciding to put it on your not-to-do list. It's not that it doesn't matter; it's just that it doesn't matter *yet*. Without a not-to-do list, the only place for it to go is on top of your ever-growing list of to-dos, and that doesn't help. Sure, from time to time you'll pull more into a week because you wind up with more space than expected, but that's an exception, not the rule.

At this point you may be thinking, *OK, great, I have a not-to-do list now, but I can't just ignore whatever the week throws at me once I get into it.* I agree. The purpose of upfront clarity is to help you be more intentional throughout the week. So let's take a look at how to use your not-to-do list to keep you focused as the inevitable barrage of new priorities comes your way.

Stay focused

Just between us (I promise not to tell your boss), would you ever go to work high? I hope not, but I'll share something shocking with you. Without knowing it, you're probably doing something every day that drops your performance well below what it would be if you did show up to work high. The culprit? Trying to do more than you should.

Despite what you might think, you cannot multitask. Your brain can only do one thing at a time. What feels like multitasking is actually your attention switching quickly back and forth between tasks, creating the illusion that you're doing multiple things at once. Think of how a movie isn't actually moving. It's just a bunch of still pictures flashing by your eyes fast enough to create the illusion of motion.

When you try to do more than one thing at a time, you're effectively distracting yourself. The results are brutal. You get about 40 percent less work done and you get dumber too. Your IQ drops by about 10 percent when you check your messages while working—even if you're not responding. That's equivalent to the cognitive decline of losing an entire night's sleep and *twice* the impact of smoking marijuana. You're better off going to work high than knowing you have an unread email in your inbox. Please don't test this one out. The research is solid.

A distraction is basically anytime you should have said no, but didn't. To fight distractions, you have to learn to say no up front. The challenge is that you can only know if something is a distraction by comparing it to whatever else you could be doing in that moment. Answering email in a meeting is probably a distraction, but replying to that urgent request from your boss probably isn't. Your not-to-do list shines a light on potential distractions before they occur. Your to-do list gives you a comparison point to use as new requests come up throughout the week.

With your priorities (and non-priorities) defined in advance, you can respond to situations rather than blindly reacting to them. This concept is prevalent in psychology and remember: saying no to the right things at the right time is primarily a psychological challenge. When someone says something you don't like and that vein starts to bulge out of your neck while you angrily scream back, that's reacting. Talk to most psychologists and they'd recommend trying to respond instead.

Reacting is quick. Responding is slower, creating space between an event and what you do or do not choose to do. Perhaps that person didn't mean to offend you and a deep breath followed by a calm question is a better choice than your anger-fueled tirade. Prioritization is similar: when you decide what is and isn't a priority in advance, you won't simply react to any given situation. You'll make intentional choices in the moment, no matter what that moment brings.

RESPOND, DON'T REACT, TO POTENTIAL NEW WORK THROUGHOUT YOUR WEEK.

As requests and tasks come up throughout the week, compare them against what you've already written down. If it's on your not-to-do list, then don't do it. If it's something you think you need to do, go for it. But before you do, choose what it will replace on your to-do list. Don't just add it on top of everything else. Move at least one to-do over to your not-to-do list. By forcing yourself to think through a trade-off before you jump into new tasks, you'll be more mindful about whether or not it's a distraction.

To help you decide if you should take on a new priority when one comes up, ask yourself:

- Is this new thing more impactful than what I already have planned?
- Does this new thing unblock or unlock more people or work than what I already have planned?
- Is it already on my not-to-do list? If so, what's different to justify a change?

I use a simple framework to make these decisions in the moment:

What to Do with a New Task?

Higher Impact

Do it later
Add it to your not-to-do
list for another week

Make it a big bet
Move an existing top
priority to your not-to-do

Enables Less ← → Enables More

Ignore
Don't do these

Add it to your to-do list
Move at least one to-do
to your not-to-do

Lower Impact

The key concept here is to force a trade-off. Though you may have to add more on top of your existing priorities at times, make that option a last resort rather than a regular reaction. If you decide not to take on the new task, you can always add it to your not-to-do list to be prioritized for another week. Essentially, your not-to-do list becomes the holding area for everything important you plan to get to later. You can decide what, if anything, moves from your not-to-do list one week to your to-do list the next.

Now, let's discuss possibly the hardest part of saying yes to more no.

How to get more comfortable saying no

Saying no to others is scary. Yet to take back control of your time, you need to learn to say no confidently and reasonably—and without sounding like a jerk.

The secret is to involve others. One reason you spent the time above to get clarity on your priorities and non-priorities is so that you can share it with others when you need to say no to them. When you don't have your own up-front clarity, you likely won't feel good about saying no. On the other hand, when you're able to tell people what you're prioritizing (and not prioritizing) and why, you're better equipped to offer a reasonable no. This is where the final, key step in saying no well comes into play.

Instead of offering a blunt no, share your prioritization and *ask their opinion*.

The beauty of this approach is that it turns an emotional situation into a more comfortable, analytical one. Together, you and the other person can discuss the merits of how you're thinking about your prioritization and where their new request fits in. Ask them if they think you're wrong about your priorities. Allow them to share their feedback. Then decide whether your no needs to stand or your priorities need to change.

When you take this approach, it's less about the fear of how someone might react and more about responding to what they actually say. You can't have this kind of conversation if you only have one long to-do list. Everything looks important. That's why you wrote a not-to-do list at the beginning of the week.

INSTEAD OF SAYING NO, ASK "WHAT DO YOU THINK?"

This approach works because you're giving others the opportunity to collaborate on the no when it's needed. They can hear you out on your thinking and then contribute their own opinion. Very often, they'll agree with your prioritization and say no to themselves. At other times, you'll see a change is needed and you'll say yes, knowing the change was justified. Sometimes you'll disagree and you'll have to say no, but it stings less because the other person understands why.

Here are three specific approaches you can use to more easily say no by involving others:

- "I'm prioritizing XYZ, which feels most impactful for me to do right now. Do you see it differently?"
- "I'm prioritizing XYZ right now. What would happen if I got back to you on this by Monday instead?"
- "I'm prioritizing XYZ right now. Do you know of anyone else that could help?"

If after trying these you still find yourself stuck, your manager or project lead can be a helpful next step. Bring them the competing priorities and use the questions above to get their input. If the challenge is with your manager, ask them what other priorities could come off your plate to help you focus on getting the new work done and see what they say.

Too good to be true

Katharine made a full recovery and never returned to that restaurant. She eventually shared her story with me about her month with salmonella. When she did, we agreed she needed a prioritization intervention. Together we walked through the concepts that ultimately became the backbone for this chapter. She leaned hard into clarifying her not-to-dos in advance, even setting one not to work past 4 p.m. during her first week back to make sure she didn't overdo it.

If you want to take back control of your time and save up to a full day every week by avoiding distractions, you need to learn to say no more effectively. It's really hard to say no, and that's why most of us don't do it as much as we should.

You can say no to the right things at the right times by doing the following:

1. Write a not-to-do list before the week starts to avoid overplanning, overworking, and the overwhelming feeling of too many priorities.
2. Then, when requests and new potential work come up throughout the week, respond, don't react, to consciously decide whether it's a distraction.
3. Finally, make it easier to say no to others (and avoid sounding like a jerk) by asking for their opinion on your priorities.

Shift your mindset toward what not to do and how not to do it. You'll get more done and feel better about it along the way.

And always, always, always remember to say no to the discount lunch special.

ACTION EXERCISE

Write a not-to-do list for your week. Take whatever to-do list you have right now and:

1. Pick your top three most important priorities.
2. Put everything else on your not-to-do list. *Yes, everything else.*
3. Only add more to your to-do list if your schedule is wide open after blocking out time for your top three priorities.

Do this now and each Monday for at least the next two weeks. At the end of two weeks, reflect on the experience:

- What did you intentionally not do each week? How did it help you make progress on what you did do?
- Were you able to say no to others? Why or why not?

Further reading in case you feel like it

- *Essentialism: The Disciplined Pursuit of Less*, Greg McKeown— All about how to focus on the few essential things that matter most so you can have maximum impact without spreading yourself too thin.

- *Four Thousand Weeks*, Oliver Burkeman—You're not here for long. This book covers strategies to help you make the most of the limited time you have.

- *Deep Work*, Cal Newport—The benefits of uninterrupted work and how to avoid distractions so you can focus.

How to Do 5 Days of Work in 4
(Without Working until Midnight)

Chapter 1 **How to eliminate miscommunication**

Miscommunications cost you almost a full day every single week. The key to stopping them so you can start saving your time and frustration is about listening, not speaking.

- *Asking for a brief back:* "Can you let me know what you took away from this conversation so I can be sure I did a good job getting my point across?"
- *Giving a brief back:* "I think what you just told me is [insert the message you heard]. Did I get that right?"

Chapter 2 **How to speed up slow decision-making**

Unnecessarily slow decision-making on your team costs you over a full day every single week. You can get that time back and decide faster by disagreeing better (without trying to agree).

1. Ask "Who is deciding?" before debating any decision.
2. Share context, not opinions, in order to avoid groupthink.
3. Seek alignment, not agreement, to move forward even when you can't agree.

Chapter 3 **How to take back control of your time**

You say yes to distractions because it's hard to say no, costing you up to a day per week. Avoid distractions and reclaim the time you need to finish your own work by writing a not-to-do list.

1.   Put your top three most important priorities on your to-do list.
2.   Put everything else on your not-to-do list.
3.   Only add more to your to-do list if your schedule is wide open after blocking out time for your top three priorities.

Use your not-to-do list to ask for feedback on your priorities when a new to-do arises.

PART 2

How to Enjoy Your Day-to-Day Work More (Without Changing Jobs)

Each of the tactics we just covered will help you save time. Using them all together can save you upward of a full day every single week without decreasing how much you get done. The only question now is, what do you want to do with all your newfound time?

Conventional wisdom says to always start any self-improvement by looking within. Great advice, but who has the time for that? Well, now you do.

Turns out that one of the best ways to do better at your job is to enjoy your work more. The challenge is that most of us don't feel we have enough agency to make meaningful changes. The truth is that you have more control than you think, and you don't need to change your job to enjoy it more.

In Part 2, we'll focus on how to help you get out of your own way. We'll dive into one of the most frustrating psychological challenges

UNLOCK

you face at work and then rethink how you do your job day-to-day. You'll learn to see the control you do have and tactics for applying it to enjoy your job even more than you do today. Each of the following three chapters is based on a common misconception, with an unconventional conclusion:

- **Chapter 4:** Self-doubt is a superpower—and how to tap into it.

- **Chapter 5:** You're looking for joy on the job in all the wrong places—and where to look instead.

- **Chapter 6:** You have more control over work than you might think—and how to put it to work for you.

Ever feel like you can't measure up to your team or the task at hand? Think you know what makes you happy at work? Think enjoying your job is great for everyone else, but not for you? Let me show you why you should think again.

IT'S NOT A SYNDROME

How to Promote the Imposter in You

I have written 11 books, but each time I think, 'Uh oh, they're going to find out now. I've run a game on everybody, and they're going to find me out.'

—MAYA ANGELOU

"Why would anyone on this team take me seriously?"

Sarah is a high achiever. She has a PhD in biological chemistry and had been promoted twice in three years at the medical diagnostic company she worked for. She also had a track record of getting things done, and that's why her CEO approached her directly to take on a new project. One of the company's most critical technical teams was struggling. Sarah's CEO wanted her to figure out why and help fix whatever was going wrong. That's what prompted Sarah to share her self-doubt with me.

We'd been working together for a few months, and her honest question took me by surprise. Despite her many achievements, Sarah didn't feel like she belonged. As a scientist and not an engineer, she didn't see how she could help the team with their increasingly more complicated technical discussions. Once she finished telling me all the ways she didn't measure up to her new teammates, I asked her, "What should you do next?"

She replied, "Ask to move to a new team."

"Sure, that's one option. What else could you do?"

She raised an eyebrow. "Study engineering as quickly as possible?"

I laughed, but I wasn't going to let her off that easily. "OK. What else?"

She paused, then sighed. "I'm not sure, but I don't see how I will keep up with this team. They're really smart."

I let the silence sit and then said, "Why don't you ask for feedback *about yourself* from your team, the people you don't think will take you seriously, and see what they say?"

I thought it would help her to hear what they really thought of her. Good or bad, at least the feedback would be specific and we could work on whatever she heard. Reluctantly, Sarah agreed.

When we met two weeks later, she told me that one of her colleagues had said, "Our team has gotten better since you joined it. You help us think critically about the challenges we face, and you often share helpful perspectives we haven't thought about."

That's stellar feedback! Anyone would be happy to hear something like that about themselves. Except Sarah wasn't happy. Sure, she appreciated the kind words, but the praise only made her feel more pressure. She glossed over the positivity and instead focused on how she wouldn't be able to live up to everyone's high expectations of her.

She felt like an imposter.

She didn't want to shy away from the challenge, but she definitely needed a change. What Sarah was feeling is commonly called *imposter syndrome*, and she was on the verge of letting it get the better of her. She was looking for any way to make it stop.

Like Sarah, when you feel the self-doubt of imposter syndrome, you might see it as a problem. That you need to get rid of your insecurity to do and feel better. Common advice talks about imposter syndrome like it's something you need to overcome. Just "believe in yourself." After all, "You can do anything you put your mind to." These sayings don't help. When you have doubts, you probably try to ignore them. I'll bet that doesn't work. Imposter syndrome isn't a light switch you can turn on and off. When you try to ignore the feeling that you don't belong, it usually feels worse and you perform worse as well. That's why we're going to completely flip the script.

By the end of this chapter, you'll know how to use the same imposter syndrome that feels like it's holding you back as the very thing that propels you toward more impact and a deeper feeling that *you do belong*.

We're all imposters

You've experienced imposter syndrome if you've ever:
- felt self-doubt,
- had trouble acknowledging your success, or
- been worried that you'll be exposed as a fraud because you're not as good as other people think you are.

The textbook definition of imposter syndrome adds that these feelings happen despite verifiable and objective evidence of your success. Sound familiar?

When you hear positive feedback like Sarah's, do you believe it? Can you think of a time when positive feedback later made you feel *worse* because you were worried that sooner or later you'd let everyone down?

Though imposter syndrome can lead to more serious depression and anxiety in some cases (if you're experiencing debilitating negativity, speaking to a trained mental health professional is the best course of action), the more moderate versions most of us experience day-to-day can still be significantly challenging. Even if you push through it, the effort of constantly battling any nagging negativity creates emotional overhead that leads to burnout. In this chapter, I'll help you prevent self-doubt from getting to that point in the first place and share an approach to transform your very normal, albeit negative, thoughts into a positive driver for you.

Start by relaxing. If you're an imposter, so am I. I'm sitting here, right now, writing these words, thinking I couldn't possibly write a "real" book. It's not just me and you, either. It's pretty much everyone else you know too. Research shows that for every ten people, more than eight have or will experience imposter syndrome at some point in their careers. You really are not alone on this one.

In fact, Dr. Pauline Rose Clance, the psychologist and professor who first discovered and studied imposter syndrome, spent years thinking she was the only one feeling like she didn't belong. It wasn't until one of her top students came to her one day and said, "I feel like an imposter here with all these really bright people" that she knew there was something bigger than her own feelings she needed to understand. She kicked off research with her colleague, Dr. Suzanne Imes, and in 1978 they published their findings, describing what they called *imposter phenomenon*. Since then, thousands of studies, papers, and books have been published building on their initial research. To her frustration, the name has drifted from imposter phenomenon to full-blown imposter *syndrome*, but to her credit, many of the same basic principles have stood the test of time.

What not to do

When you feel like an imposter, you probably can't just switch it off and ignore it. That's because imposter syndrome is a feeling, and most feelings are rarely rational. Roughly 40 percent of people have a fear of flying despite it statistically being far safer than driving to and from work every day. If you're afraid of flying, or sit next to someone on a flight who is, simply explaining how infrequently planes have crashed in the past isn't going to help. Imposter syndrome is the same. Like Sarah, knowing that you've been successful in the past doesn't make you feel better. Past success is more of a prerequisite than a prevention for imposter syndrome. Rational analysis doesn't make it any easier to deal with.

In fact, when you try to turn your self-doubt off, you usually wind up feeling worse. That's why I think Dr. Clance is frustrated that it's become known as a syndrome. You start with a few normal negative thoughts that most people experience, and instead of addressing those for what they are, you feel worse because now you also have a "syndrome" to deal with. All of a sudden, there's something wrong with you that you have to fix, and it feels even worse when you can't.

Stop trying to fix it.

There's more to imposter syndrome than what prevailing wisdom would have you believe. It's not some bug in your source code that needs to be corrected. It's a feature to be embraced. When you stop trying to turn it off, imposter syndrome can bring you benefits rather than burnout.

From syndrome to superpower

The specific nature of imposter syndrome makes it a potential superpower. It's obviously about you, but at its core, imposter syndrome is really about other people. It seems to be a special case of a fear of failure, and not just that we might mess something up. We all make mistakes, and that seems to be less of a big deal. Imposter syndrome zooms in on the very specific fear that you don't belong on your team and can't measure up to your peers. The key to unlocking the benefits of imposter syndrome is about better leveraging its focus on belonging.

Dr. Basima Tewfik is a professor at MIT's Sloan School of Management who literally got her doctorate in imposter syndrome. Looking to understand the broader picture about imposter syndrome, she ran multiple studies on both its positive and negative impacts. She found that the story goes much deeper than it purely being a bad feeling, as most people would assume. Imposter syndrome has its benefits, says Dr. Tewfik, and like Dr. Clance, she seems to object to it being labeled as a syndrome. Clearly, we're in need of a major rebrand here.

In one study, she hired trained actors to present specific diseases in simulated appointments with doctors who believed they were taking part in a training exercise. She found that the doctors with *imposter thoughts* (her preferred term for syndrome) performed just as well in terms of their clinical diagnoses as their counterparts without self-doubt. So feeling like an imposter wasn't negatively impacting their job performance. The imposter doctors were, however, rated as better than their more self-confident counterparts in post "appointment" reviews from their "patients."

Overall, Dr. Tewfik's research has shown that when you experience imposter syndrome, you tend to compensate by becoming more "other-focused." You listen better and ask more questions. When you do, you become more interpersonally effective and people like working with you more. In other words, the very concerns you have about not belonging help you build more belonging. The right amount of imposter syndrome makes you a better teammate.

Dr. Basima Tewfik said this about her findings:

> "To date, there's no empirical quantitative evidence that imposter thoughts degrade performance. Yet this notion persists... It may be that having the right amount of imposter thoughts can provide just enough motivation to bring out your best work."

Dr. Tewfik cautions against intentionally thinking as many negative thoughts as possible just to build better relationships. Instead, she wants her work to show that there is much more to imposter syndrome than the purely negative press it tends to receive. There's a right amount of imposter syndrome, and that right amount is likely not zero. Surprisingly, you shouldn't try to completely turn off your imposter thoughts.

DO NOT TRY TO KILL YOUR IMPOSTER SYNDROME.

Imposter syndrome (or phenomenon or thoughts or perfectly normal thinking—rebrand pending) happens when you feel like you're missing something the rest of your team has, like talent or knowledge. Then, due to your self-diagnosed lack, you fear you don't belong and will be discovered as the fraud you are. To leverage imposter syndrome, you need a way to close your knowledge gap while building more belonging so you feel safe on your team. Luckily, a single tactic gives you both the context you might be missing and fosters more belonging at the same time. What is it?

I'm glad you asked, because that is both the question and the answer.

The question is the answer

To help you leverage imposter syndrome, you're going to need to get out of your head and take tangible next steps. If you don't, you risk getting stuck ruminating on your negative thoughts, which is what leads to burnout. For what action to take, we turn to the experts again, this time out of Harvard University.

Looking to understand how various interactions change how people feel about us, Dr. Alison Brooks and her colleagues at Harvard ran a number of experiments designed to study different kinds of conversations. They paired unknowing speed daters with planted actors to learn what strategies led to more second dates, scripted one side of online chats to see the different ways people would react, and observed thousands of other conversations to understand how you can best interact with other people.

Over and over, their results showed the same thing: people like you better when you ask more questions. When people like you better, you'll feel a greater sense of belonging. Despite their superpower, most of us don't recognize questions as the pathway to interpersonal success. We don't ask enough questions. Instead, we have it backward. We tend to focus more on answers, thinking this will make us seem smarter and more valuable. But answers aren't better.

At the time of this writing, Google is answering an average of about 99,000 questions every second. Even Google's answers are beginning to feel outdated with the advent of AI chatbots that answer questions in a way that feels as natural as talking to your colleague in the next cubicle. Answers are easy; they've become commoditized. When a market is completely flooded with similar products, we stop caring about the differences between them and any one will do just fine. For instance, take the gas in your car. Personally, I don't care where or what brand of gas I fill my tank with. I just care that the gas station is nearby and well priced.

For the most part, answers are like gas. They're easy to get and it doesn't really matter where they come from, so long as they get you where you want to go. What really has value in workplaces today is figuring out *the right questions to ask*. Not only do great questions pave the way for great answers, but they're also one of the best ways to learn and build relationships. That's why asking more questions is exactly the tactic you need to leverage the benefits of imposter syndrome. When you experience feelings of doubt, you don't need to push them away. Instead, recognize them as a helpful reminder to go and ask more questions.

ASKING **QUESTIONS** UNLOCKS THE BENEFITS OF IMPOSTER SYNDROME.

By asking more questions, you'll learn whatever you might be missing while building more trust and better connections with your teammates. They're the perfect tactic to deploy whenever you feel like you don't belong.

The problem is that asking questions is hard and scary. When you ask a question, you inherently expose what you don't know. Do that, and people might see you're not good enough. Thanks for that piece of cyclical reasoning imposter syndrome! We need a way to make it easier to ask more questions.

How to ask more questions

Dr. Alison Brooks and her Harvard team wanted to know more about question-asking, so they experimented with asking research participants both open-ended questions and highly specific questions. They even asked deeply uncomfortable questions like: "While an adult, have you ever felt sexual desire for a minor?" to see what would happen. Can you imagine asking anyone that question, let alone a colleague under any circumstance at work?

If you ever did (please don't), you would definitely create problems. A question like that is not going to help you in any situation, let alone with building more belonging on your team. Even though questions are the answer to empowering your imposter syndrome, you do need to make sure that you ask the right ones at the right times and in the right places. I'm pretty glad I wasn't the person on Dr. Brooks' research team who had to ask near-total strangers about their sexual preferences, and I can only imagine how it felt for the person who did. Luckily for us, they braved the tough moments so we don't have to.

When to ask questions

What they found is that follow-up questions consistently performed the best in terms of how much they make people like you. Follow-ups encourage people to elaborate on their points while showing your colleagues that you are listening to them. You can't ask a follow-up question if you weren't listening in the first place, so when you ask one, you're sending a strong signal that you were paying attention. Your colleagues will appreciate you all the more for it, and that's why the best time for you to ask a question is after listening to what someone else has said.

Follow-ups are also easier questions for you to ask because you don't have to come up with a brilliant new insight on your own. You simply listen to what others are saying and then ask them to elaborate on anything you found interesting or confusing.

THE BEST TIME TO ASK A QUESTION IS AS A **FOLLOW-UP**, AFTER LISTENING TO WHAT SOMEONE ELSE HAS SAID.

Where to ask questions

To help unpack where you should ask questions, the Harvard research team also tested the impact of varying group sizes. They showed that adding more and more people to a group didn't change how much an individual appreciates you asking them questions. It did, however, change how everyone else listening felt. Pretty much every meeting you're ever in has one or two people talking while everyone else is listening. The people talking to each other appreciate questions most. Everyone else prefers to hear answers.

It's not that questions in group settings are inherently bad. It's just that they come with more risk. It's harder, and usually scarier, to ask questions in larger group settings, and the Harvard research showed that your fear is well founded. The best, and easiest, setting for asking questions is in one-on-one conversations. If you're feeling imposter syndrome, you'll have the most success focusing on individual interactions to begin with. If you're in a big meeting and don't feel comfortable asking a question, don't ask it. Write it down and find a time to follow up with the right person.

Eventually, you can work toward becoming more comfortable in group settings, but there is no need to start there. Starting with individual conversations will help you build up your confidence to ask more questions in larger groups.

ASK QUESTIONS IN ONE-ON-ONE MEETINGS FIRST.

What questions to ask

Let's check back in with my friend Sarah. By this point, she was ready to start asking more questions—and she started with me. When she asked me for specific questions she could use, I realized it was time for my own experimentation. Over the course of a few weeks, I tried out many different kinds of follow-up questions (I stopped short of asking about sexual preferences). I found three follow-up questions I can recommend if you're not quite sure where to start.

Help me understand...

This question takes a number of different forms, such as:

- Help me understand what you mean by...
- Help me understand how you're thinking about...
- Help me understand how you're feeling about...

Asking someone to help you understand is one of my favorite questions. The language is very disarming and allows you to hone in on a specific concept or comment you'd like to know more about. It's an easy question to ask because you don't need to think up a complex, brilliantly original question. Simply listen to someone else until you get lost and then ask them to elaborate.

What do you think about...

This question usually looks something like:

- What do you think about [*insert situation here*]?
- What do you think about [*insert problem/opportunity here*]?
- What do you think about [*insert idea here*]?

Asking someone else what they think is all about fostering collaboration. You're creating space for them to bring their thinking out into the open, which they'll love. This is a great question to ask when you want to unpack someone else's perspective or learn what they think about a question, concern, or possibility you have in mind. Ask this question by listening to what someone is saying and, when a topic sparks your interest or gives you pause, ask them to tell you more.

What did we not discuss?

Near the end of a conversation, I usually ask a question that looks something like this:

- What did I *not* ask you that I should have?
- What do you think we should have talked about but didn't?
- What else do you think is important that we didn't cover?

There's usually information that doesn't naturally come up in any given conversation. I like to ask people what we did not discuss that we should have because it gives them a chance to share anything they feel we missed. I ask this question all the time and regularly find it leads to something important that would not otherwise have come up. People often tell me they appreciate being asked as well.

When not to ask questions

The ultimate goal of asking a question is to learn. Slight changes in wording will make a difference in how you make other people feel when you ask them questions, which will change what you hear back from them as a result. Though you will need to develop your own style, I do recommend following one simple rule when asking questions: ask a question with a genuine interest to understand, or don't ask it at all.

ASK A QUESTION WITH A **GENUINE INTEREST TO UNDERSTAND,** OR DON'T ASK IT AT ALL.

Great questions come from a desire to understand. Bad ones are about undermining. When I ask you to help me understand something you said with a genuine interest to learn from you, it benefits both of us. I'll gain a new understanding from you, and you'll likely gain clarity from having to collect your thinking and explain it to me in a new way. Helpful questions increase your understanding and are appreciated by those you work with.

Harmful questions are designed to show off what you already know or expose a weakness in someone else. If you ask a question with a genuine desire to increase your understanding and someone judges you negatively, so be it. If, on the other hand, you're asking a question to show off what you know or intentionally push someone else down, any negative judgment you get is well deserved. Use questions to learn. Otherwise, go another route.

If you have an opinion, state it. If you want to disagree with someone, do it. If you feel a certain way about the actions of a colleague, give them feedback. A question is not the right way to show off what you know or to passive-aggressively make a point. Questions build belonging when they come from a genuine desire to learn.

Compliment, don't compete

Once you've become comfortable asking more questions, you can start looking for other ways to contribute. One of Sarah's biggest concerns was that everyone on her team was a better engineer than her. Yet the more questions Sarah asked, the more she realized her team wasn't struggling with engineering problems. She may not have been the best engineer, but few on the team had her expertise fostering technical teamwork. This is what her colleague was talking about when they told her she brought new perspectives. They didn't need a great engineer. They had plenty of those. They needed Sarah's new thinking on how their team of great engineers could better work together.

Sarah's problem wasn't about her skill set; it was about her perspective. She was focused on what her team could do that she couldn't. She needed to be more focused on what *she* could do that they couldn't. As soon as she stopped trying to be a better engineer, she felt better.

FOCUS ON WHAT **YOU'RE GREAT AT**, NOT WHAT OTHERS CAN DO THAT YOU CAN'T.

Whether you're on a team of people with skills just like yours or working with a group where you bring a different skill set, focusing on what you uniquely bring to the table will positively shift your perspective. In Chapter 6 we'll cover how to get clear and specific about your own best way of contributing. In the meantime, the key point here is that Sarah didn't need to be a better version of her team and neither do you. Focus on being the best version of yourself.

Promoting the imposter in you

Imposter syndrome isn't all bad. In fact, you can leverage it to become a driving force in building better relationships and deeper feelings that *you do belong*. Unlike conventional advice telling you to believe in yourself, ignore your doubts, and overcome your imposter syndrome, put your imposter feelings to work for you instead. When you feel like you're not good enough or that you'll be found out as less than others think you are, use it as a trigger. When the "syndrome" hits, follow these steps:

1. Ask follow-up questions in one-on-one meetings to learn what you don't know and build stronger relationships in the process.
2. Redirect your focus from what your team does better than you to what you can uniquely bring to them.
3. Once you feel comfortable, start asking more questions in group settings so you can help get the most out of your team.

Ultimately, Sarah stopped trying to get rid of her imposter syndrome. She let herself off the hook and felt much better when she looked at the benefits imposter syndrome provided, rather than seeing it as something wrong with her. The more she felt like an imposter, the more questions she asked people. This built stronger feelings of belonging while helping her learn what she needed to know so she could find her own best way of contributing.

Within a few months of her first asking for feedback, the team had turned things around. They became much more productive, and Sarah finally felt like she belonged. After about a year, she was promoted again. When it came time to jump into that new challenge on another new team, she found her imposter syndrome had been promoted along with her. Whispers of *I'm not smart enough for this position* echoed in her mind.

The next time we met, she smiled at me and said, "I'm excited for my new role and team, but I have to admit that my imposter syndrome is creeping back in."

I was confused about why she was smiling. Apparently, my face immediately gave me away. She let the moment hang so I asked, "Well, what are you—"

She cut me off. "What am I going to do next? That's a great question."

ACTION EXERCISE

To help you get used to asking more questions before the next time your imposter syndrome hits, pick a person from your team that you admire in some way and book them for a meeting. Tell them you want to learn about how they developed a skill they have that you're interested in.

During your meeting:

- Tell them you're working on how well you ask questions.
- Ask them one or more of these follow-up questions:
  - Help me understand...
  - What do you think about...
  - What did we not talk about that we should have...
- See if they have any feedback for you about how your questions made them feel or how you can improve your question-asking in the future.

The next time you feel imposter syndrome building up, use it as a trigger. Pick at least one person, schedule a meeting, and ask them follow-up questions.

Further reading in case you feel like it

- *The Courage to Be Disliked*, Ichiro Kishimi and Fumitake Koga—Explores how to break free of one's need for approval from others. It's less tactical and more philosophical, but it's still one of my favorites.

- *How to Win Friends and Influence People*, Dale Carnegie—An oldie, but a goody. The interpersonal tactics in this book are timeless.

- *Chatter*, Ethan Kross—The psychology and neuroscience behind the voice in our head, how it can hurt you, and techniques to help you manage whatever mental chatter you might have going on.

5

MY BILLION-DOLLAR BUSINESS MISTAKE

How to Measure Your Joy on the Job

Joy's soul lies in the doing.
—SHAKESPEARE

Years ago I was invited to a meeting at Facebook to talk about growth strategies. Though the discussion itself was interesting, it was the people in the room, one in particular, who grabbed my attention. It was my first time meeting Jordan, which turned out to be a chance encounter that changed my outlook on work and life.

Jordan wasn't the most technical person in the room, but the way he carried himself as the leader of his team impressed me. I wanted to know more about his story, but we'd only just met. Fortunately, my boss at the time knew him well and later put us in touch. I asked if I could buy him a coffee and was surprised when he invited me back to Facebook's office in a few weeks for a one-on-one. Since I had time before our meeting, I researched him.

That's when I got nervous.

Jordan is Jordan Banks. You may not know his name, but to say he's a heavy-hitter in tech is to undersell his influence across a vast array of properties you likely use. He was an early employee at eBay and was then hired by Sheryl Sandberg at the beginning of her tenure at Facebook. He's served on multiple boards of directors. Run more than one company. Has a degree in law. He's smart, well-connected, and others speak highly of him. It's no wonder that he's been named "The Most Influential Innovator in Canada" and one of "Canada's 50 Most Powerful Business People."

It gets worse.

Aside from being successful in business, he's also a highly present father, a generous donor to the causes he cares about like geriatric care and children's hospitals, *and* he takes time to talk to young, wide-eyed go-getters about their quests to do all the big things he's done in life. When I was twenty-something, he was the epitome of success I wanted (to be honest, he still is).

Now you have the same baggage I had when I met Jordan for our chat. Facebook Canada had just moved into a new, sleek office building complete with all the Canadian clichés, including a phone booth designed to look like a hockey penalty box. While I waited for Jordan to finish his previous meeting, his executive assistant offered to take me on a tour of the office. As I walked past the buffet and newly installed wall of printed Instagram photos (Facebook had only recently completed its acquisition of Instagram), I couldn't help but notice the *hundreds* of employees who all seemed incredibly busy. I rarely get nervous meeting new people, but I had a stark realization during that quick tour: *Jordan is in charge of all of this. Every person here wants his time, yet he's giving an hour to me. Do not blow it, Jason.*

Fortunately, I had a list of questions prepared:

- How did you get this job? Your former job?
- What's your biggest challenge here? How did you overcome it?
- How do you make career decisions?

Ultimately, every boring question was an unsubtle way of asking, "How can I become you on the shortest path possible?" When we met, I (thankfully) didn't even get to ask my questions. After some small talk, Jordan asked, "What do you want to do?"

I didn't hesitate. "I want to run a billion-dollar business."

I'd said that to others before. Almost without fail, the people I told would immediately push back with every rational reason why I couldn't do that: too inexperienced, not enough skills, etc. Jordan didn't flinch. In so many words he said, "Sure, you could do that. But do you really want to? Are you going to enjoy yourself?"

I had no immediate answer. I was so prepared to argue what I would do to achieve that level of success that I'd overlooked an essential part of the problem: how I'd feel along the way. My enjoyment didn't matter. Just the outcome. I'd enjoy that when I got there.

In the awkward silence that followed, Jordan kept pressing his point. "Have you thought about what running a billion-dollar business will feel like? How is that going to change your life? What kind of work will you have to do to get there? Are you even interested in doing that work? Is that the kind of lifestyle you want to have?"

I may not have physically bristled against his questions during our meeting, but I caught myself internally retaliating. *That's easy for you to say, Jordan. You're there, at the end of the path I want to follow.*

After some time reflecting on our meeting, I realized why he was asking me such specific questions. His successful career could be attributed to many variables, but one constant remained: he'd made methodical decisions prioritizing his experience at work, not just his expected return.

I was narrowly focused on achievement and ambition. Jordan was trying to show me that my experience was a much better compass. This isn't the well-worn mantra about how if you do what you love, you'll never work a day in your life. Work is hard; that's why it isn't called *play*. Even if you love your job, you're bound to hate it at times. Instead, this is about taking some of the monumental attention you put on your ambition and the milestones you hope to achieve and focusing it on how you want to feel along the way—watering the grass you already have so it becomes greener, so to speak. It's about systematically increasing your joy on the job no matter how much you do or don't love your work today.

I'll show you exactly how to do that, but first, let me start with a question of my own: Do you enjoy your job?

The more you enjoy, the better you do

Enjoying what you do at work isn't just important because it feels good. Research has shown that when you enjoy your job, you have more impact, are more creative, and you build better relationships with your colleagues. Enjoying your day-to-day work is a self-reinforcing multiplier for your career. The more you enjoy your job, the more impact you have. The more impact you have, the more you'll enjoy your job. And so it goes, onward and upward from there.

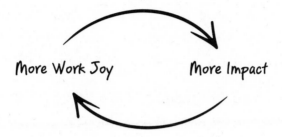

Work joy also spills outside of the office into your life overall. When you feel good at work, you feel better across the rest of your life as well. Just imagine not carrying the stress of your work home with you. Better yet, when you're no longer simply making it through your days at the office, picture how much more energy you'll have for everything else in your life. Enjoying your job is a shortcut to thriving both at work and outside of it.

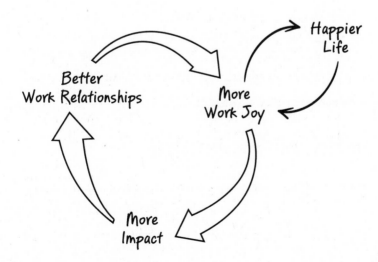

The best part? Enjoyment, like all feelings, is limitless. There's no ceiling on how much you can enjoy your job. No matter how much you love or hate it today, you can always enjoy your job more. Whether you're trying to get out of a funk or enjoy a job you already love even more, systematically improving your day-to-day experience can bring endless gains to your impact. The less your work drains you, the more it will positively drive your life.

In the last chapter we covered how to put imposter syndrome to work for you, so it no longer works against you. Now that you have one of the most common causes of negativity out of your way, the path is clear for you to improve your job itself. Don't worry if you feel like you really need your paycheck and enjoying your work is a luxury you simply can't afford. We're not going to touch your job. Instead, we'll explore how you can take a different approach to the work you already have to do. By the end of this chapter, you'll have a new way to look at your day-to-day experience. You'll also learn a new tactic to help you better understand exactly what you do and do not enjoy doing, which you'll then use in the following chapter to change how you're working for the better.

Let's start by going back to my question: Do you enjoy your job? That question is much harder than it sounds. What if I told you that you're thinking about it all wrong?

You're measuring the wrong variable

Think winning the lottery will make you happy? Think again. In a classic study showing just how poor our intuition is for what actually makes us happy, a group of researchers from Northwestern

University and the University of Massachusetts showed that winning the lottery did not really make people feel happier. Sure, they had a momentary high after winning and the shopping sprees that followed, but before long they got used to their new normal and found something else to stress about. Their overall happiness mostly returned to whatever it had been before all the money. There's a phrase for that phenomenon, and it isn't limited to lottery winners. We all experience it in one form or another.

Hedonic adaptation is our shared, human tendency to revert to a base level of happiness following any meaningful event. Like getting a big promotion or landing that fancy new job you've always wanted, winning the lottery is a milestone. Just think about your last major win at your job. I bet you felt great. Did you feel the same way the next day? The next week? At your next performance review? That's hedonic adaptation at work—and it's why milestones are the wrong variable to focus on.

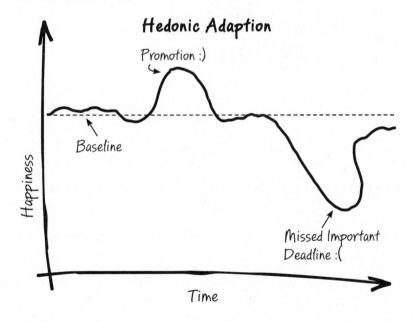

The good news about hedonic adaptation is that it means your failures won't hurt for as long as you might think. However, it also means that you're unlikely to experience real, lasting enjoyment at work if you only base how you feel on accomplishing whatever your next big goal might be.

The same study on lottery winners compared the happiness of the newly rich to recently paralyzed accident victims. Maybe by now the results won't surprise you. The accident victims were happier people. Unlike their substantially luckier counterparts, accident victims enjoyed their everyday moments more. I firmly believe that anyone can experience more joy in their job, but we have to flip our notions of what leads to more enjoyment.

HAPPINESS IS MEASURED IN **MOMENTS, NOT MILESTONES.**

Generally, we all focus on career milestones. You think about the goals you want to achieve, the promotions you plan to land, and the projects you'll need to work on to get there. Conventional wisdom says to zoom out and assess whether or not you're tracking toward your next major milestone. Based on your progress, you'll have your answer about how happy you are at work. Without addressing your day-to-day experience, however, when you get a new job, accomplish a goal, or reach an important milestone, the highs you feel always fade. If you want lasting happiness and more joy on the job, you have to focus on improving how you work, not just what you're working on.

Unfortunately, most companies have it backward. They emphasize your outcomes over your experiences. Just think about your last performance review. Did you talk more about your accomplishments or what it *felt* like to work toward them day-to-day? Don't get me wrong, hitting milestones and having performance reviews is important, but they will not result in substantially increasing your day-in, day-out joy on the job. Think of it this way: Does hitting a milestone matter to you if you're miserable making it happen?

In fact, I believe too few of us consider our work joy as often as we should. But perhaps you won the work lottery and have a great manager who's recently asked if you're enjoying your job. Or maybe you've heard questions like the ones Jordan asked me and have stopped to broadly consider how much you're enjoying your job these days. Or maybe while you're reading this chapter, you're questioning whether you're truly happy with your work. Unfortunately, there's a good chance you don't actually know how you're feeling.

Do you enjoy your moments?

When you're asked "Do you enjoy your job?" your brain plays a trick on you. A growing body of literature shows that humans are quite inaccurate at recalling how they've felt in the past. It's called *affect recall bias*. In one of many studies on the topic to date, Alberto Prati from the University of Oxford and Claudia Senik from the

Paris School of Economics analyzed data from over 60,000 adults over almost sixty years. Every day, participants would record their happiness in a diary. Then every few months, the researchers would survey each participant and ask them to reflect on how they'd felt in the past. Sometimes they reported feeling better than a later comparison with their daily diaries suggested. At other times, they remembered their pasts as worse than they were. Either way, their longer-term reflections were consistently wrong.

This is another reason why traditional performance reviews don't help you do anything about your on-the-job experience. Broad reflections over long time periods don't match how you actually feel about your work day-to-day. If you really want to know if you're enjoying your job, you need to measure your moments and ask yourself how you're feeling as close to your day-to-day experience as possible. That's exactly what two researchers from the London School of Economics were looking to do when they conducted one of the most comprehensive studies on moment-based human happiness.

To help them understand how people truly felt as they went about their daily lives, the researchers created an app and recruited tens of thousands of people to use it. The app randomly notified its users three to five times throughout their days, both inside and outside of the office, and asked them to stop and provide answers to these questions:

- What are you doing?
- Who are you doing it with?
- How happy do you feel on a scale from 0 (not at all) to 10 (completely happy)?

They collected millions of responses over more than six years and categorized what they heard into forty different activities, creating a comprehensive list of what we spend our time doing. I wasn't surprised when I saw "having sex" at the top of the list of what makes people happiest. (It was surprising to me, however, that tens of thousands of people were willing to stop *in the act* and tell an app what they were doing and who they were doing it with.)

Want to guess where work fell on the list of activities? Not dead last, but close. Work came in second to last, just barely beating out lying sick in bed. In other words, their comprehensive data on happiness showed that many of us are happier waiting in line, running errands, or doing household chores than we are while at work.

Ouch.

When I first read about this research, I didn't believe it. I decided to try it out for myself and hacked together my own version of their app. I set a regularly recurring calendar reminder to notify me throughout my day and linked it to a Google form with the three questions to fill out. At the time, I would have told you that I was happy overall. I liked my job. Sure, there were hard moments, but day-to-day I felt things were pretty good. In retrospect it seems obvious, but back then I was surprised to see that my momentary measurements painted a different picture.

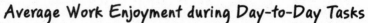

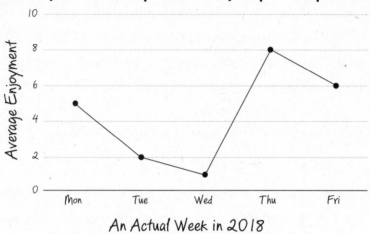

Average Work Enjoyment during Day-to-Day Tasks

An Actual Week in 2018

Immediately, you can tell I wasn't enjoying my job much that week. Worse, that week wasn't an outlier. This is what most of my weeks looked like. I thought I liked my job, but it wasn't until I asked myself how I was doing in my moments that I realized something was off. Before you can improve your experience at work, you first need to have a real understanding of how you feel about it today. Longer-term reflections, like quarterly or yearly performance reviews that focus on milestones and how they made you feel in the past, don't really help. To increase your happiness at work, you need to measure your moments.

How to measure your moments

For a comprehensive scientific study, you probably need to do hourly measurements. In real life, on the other hand, getting interrupted multiple times every day to report on what you're doing and how it's feeling is annoying and impractical. You're already distracted enough by email, meetings, and the hundreds of other things that come up throughout your day, let alone adding in a persistent reminder to share your feelings. You could repeat the moment-based research yourself, but I don't recommend it. There's a much better way that only requires about fifteen minutes at the end of your week.

After peppering me with questions and seeing what I'm sure was the deer-in-headlights look in my eyes, Jordan knew I needed something more tangible. He ran me through an exercise that I've modified over the years to help anyone measure their moments. This quick practice will clearly show you what you enjoy at your job and how much time you spend doing those things. It's simple yet effective and won't require you to report on your sex life (unless you're into that kind of thing).

I find it's best to do this on a Friday, but any day will work. Grab a pen and a single piece of blank paper, then:

1. Fold your paper in half lengthwise. You should be looking at a tall, skinny, folded piece of blank paper.

2. List the work-related tasks you enjoy doing.

3. Flip the page over so the side you just wrote on is facing down. You should be looking at another tall, skinny, folded piece of blank paper.

4. Open up your calendar. List what you actually spent your time doing this week.

5. Unfold the paper. You should now be looking at your lists side by side.

6. Draw a line from each task of enjoyment to each matching, actual task you did over the past week.

7. Now answer: "Do you enjoy your job?"

Here's an old version of one of mine from shortly after my less-than-stellar, but highly informative, week above:

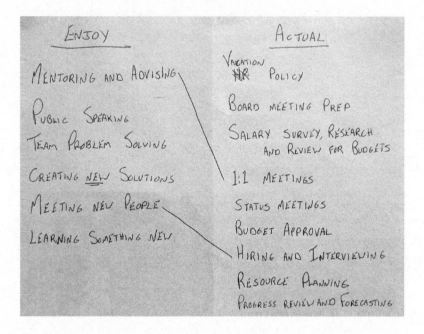

ENJOY

MENTORING AND ADVISING

PUBLIC SPEAKING
TEAM PROBLEM SOLVING

CREATING NEW SOLUTIONS

MEETING NEW PEOPLE

LEARNING SOMETHING NEW

ACTUAL

VACATION
HR POLICY

BOARD MEETING PREP

SALARY SURVEY, RESEARCH
AND REVIEW FOR BUDGETS

1:1 MEETINGS

STATUS MEETINGS

BUDGET APPROVAL

HIRING AND INTERVIEWING

RESOURCE PLANNING

PROGRESS REVIEW AND FORECASTING

Again, it's pretty clear that I wasn't spending much time doing what I enjoy. When you do this exercise for yourself, don't worry if you don't have many connecting lines. The point is to bring clarity to wherever you are now, not to make you feel bad for being off from where you might want to be later. Taking time to list out activities you enjoy will help you better understand what you like doing at work. Matching those activities up against what you actually spent your time doing over the course of the past week will answer whether or not you enjoy your day-to-day job.

If you're worried that you had a particularly great (or bad) week, simply repeat this exercise for another week or two to give you an average baseline. You're going to use this information in the next chapter to help you spend more and more time doing what you already enjoy doing. That way, whether you're currently looking at two disconnected lists or a mishmash of many lines, you can build on whatever your foundation may be.

More than what's on the page

Happiness is measured in your moments. When you rely entirely on achievements to enjoy your job, you'll feel good from time to time, but it won't last. Once I was better able to measure my moments, I could clearly see I needed a change. I just didn't know what to do about it *because I didn't know what was in my control*. I remember thinking that my feelings at work didn't matter...I just had to do what needed to be done. This is a trap too many of us fall into.

Had I known this earlier in my career, I would have accomplished what I needed to, but I would have done it differently and enjoyed myself more. And, like I've said, the more joy you have, the more impact will follow. You'll always have some work to do that you don't enjoy doing, but when you learn how to approach your work differently, you'll set a higher baseline for your joy on the job—which brings me back to Jordan Banks.

Jordan could have run any of the multibillion-dollar companies he's worked for. He has the skills, the connections, and the leadership. Instead of focusing solely on what he wanted to achieve, he asked himself how he wanted to *feel* doing any of those jobs, and purposefully chose *not* to pursue them. He knew the overlooked value of moments over milestones. When you put more attention on how you work instead of only focusing on what work you need to accomplish, you'll not only feel better, you'll do better too.

Don't believe me? Go look up Jordan Banks's Wikipedia page.

ACTION EXERCISE

Schedule fifteen minutes at the end of your day this Friday to measure your moments this week.

1. Fold a piece of paper in half lengthwise to create two columns.
2. On one side, write a list of tasks you enjoy doing.
3. On the other side, write a list of everything you actually did this week—referencing your calendar as needed.
4. Unfold the paper and draw a line from tasks you enjoy to any tasks you actually did this week.
5. Then answer: "Do you enjoy your job?"

Regardless of what you learn, pick one thing from your list of what you enjoy doing and do it tomorrow—even if just for a few minutes.

Further reading in case you feel like it

- *Stumbling on Happiness*, Daniel Gilbert—Explains the psychology of how your mind works, why it's hard to predict how you'll feel in the future, and challenges common assumptions about what makes you happy. Lots of great takeaways in this book.

- *10% Happier*, Dan Harris—This is the best introduction to meditation that I know of. It's not woo-woo at all; the author is a skeptic and his stories are hilarious.

- *The Happiness Equation: Want Nothing + Do Anything = Have Everything*, Neil Pasricha—The title does a lot of work on this one. The book isn't specifically about work, but there are lots of great happiness tactics.

DON'T UNSUBSCRIBE FROM YOURSELF

How to Unlock More Joy at Your Job

The little things? The little moments? They aren't little.

—JON KABAT-ZINN

"You gotta be kidding me!"

Now, I don't know for a fact if Megan said that, thought that, or felt that, but I have to imagine a similar line crossed her mind when she opened her inbox to find it flooded with hundreds of unwanted sales emails. While I wasn't there to witness this event, I picture Megan pushing her keyboard away, pushing back from her desk, and possibly pushing her fist through a wall. Actually, that's what I would have done in her situation.

Megan and I worked closely together for years while we were building an artificial intelligence company from the ground up. It had been a while since we last connected and as we updated each other on our lives, I told her I was writing this book. That's when she launched into her email story. Only it wasn't really a story about email.

What made her spam-filled inbox worse was that she knew the sender quite well. Megan had email-bombed herself. In a failed test of an upcoming email campaign, she accidentally sent every one of the messages to her own address—landing her in the seldom-seen situation of wanting to unsubscribe from herself.

As is often the case, Megan's issue was the result of a much larger problem that had begun many weeks before. The self-initiated avalanche of emails was just the final nudge that made it clear to her that something had to change—and soon. At the time, Megan was a newly hired salesperson at a Silicon Valley company that was beginning to make a name for itself on a global scale. Although she had been a successful management consultant, an early-stage startup executive, and an advocate for women in leadership, she'd never had a role focused entirely on sales. When she applied for the job, she was looking for a new challenge and the work sounded promising. She later told me, "I was jumping into a new role in a new market with a new product doing a new job I had never done before." But her excitement for the possibilities of what she could accomplish soon evaporated.

Early on, she was asked to build a pipeline of prospective customers. Since she was new to the company, she attended training and followed others' best practices. And because she's studious and driven, this led to her diving headfirst into learning a commonly used tool that automates customer communications. The tool replaces manual back-and-forth emails with a prewritten, automated email sequence. Megan spent weeks attempting to implement it. All told, her efforts netted exactly zero potential customers. And then the day arrived when she checked her email and said (allegedly), "You gotta be kidding me!"

Though email-bombing yourself is a laughable offense (in hindsight), Megan's issue was indicative of a square peg attempting to fit into a round hole. It was clear how misaligned her abilities and personality were from her position on paper and what she was being asked to do. Here's the context you're missing about Megan: she thrives when engaging with people.

Do you see the disconnect? Rather than seeking ways to accomplish her goals by means of doing what she enjoys and is great at, she spent countless hours *alone* tinkering with automated emails. She wasn't enjoying herself, and unsurprisingly, her results showed it. The tool wasn't working for her, and frankly neither was the job. She dreaded going to work. She wondered if she'd made the wrong decision taking the job and if she should start looking for a new one.

But her job wasn't the problem.

It's not your job. It's you.

Anyone can learn to love their job more. It doesn't matter if you love it or hate it right now, you can always enjoy what you do day-to-day even more. Just writing that out, I can almost hear you sighing. The kind of sigh that says, "That sounds good in theory." Stick with me here.

The reason why many people don't like their work as much as they could is because they're not doing their work in the best way *for them*.

Oftentimes we blame our jobs when work isn't going well. Maybe your job isn't the right fit for you, or your work isn't fun. Perhaps you need to find a new project, new team, or a new job entirely. The truth of the matter is that you can accomplish all of your tasks and goals—and with more joy and impact—if you start focusing more on *how* you work than what you're working on. Forget working on best practices. You need to find the practices that work best for you. When you do, you can use what you're already great at to find more enjoyment in the job you already have.

In the previous chapter, we explored your daily activities because that's where real, lasting enjoyment comes from—and the more you enjoy your job, the better you do at it. We unpacked how milestones feel great for a short while, but if you really want to love what you do, you need to focus on your moments. Contrary to popular belief, a dream job isn't something you get, it's something you practice.

YOU DON'T GET A DREAM JOB, YOU **PRACTICE IT**.

The challenge is that remembering to practice your own best practices is hard. I don't know many people who wake up every day determined to get their jobs done in the hardest, most painful ways. You aren't trying to get away from your best path, but when you aren't intentional about how you work, that's exactly what happens. As pressures, deadlines, and avalanches of unwanted emails pile up, you slowly drift away from what you enjoy and do really well toward the way everyone else does their jobs, even when that's not best for you.

By the end of this chapter, you'll have a tactic to define your own unique *how* and tips to keep it top of mind for any task you have to do. You'll learn to better align how you work with whatever work you have to do—and enjoy it more along the way too.

Sound like something you can subscribe to?

What are the best practices *for you*?

In considering your own joy on the job today, how often do you align your interests with accomplishing your goals? Put another way, do you consider alternative ways to meet your milestones that would bring you more happiness while you work? Remember: Megan needed to build a sales pipeline, not implement an email tool. The tool was just one of many possible paths, and it was certainly possible for her to find another way. But she was following the best-practice recommendations for her position, assuming that would lead to the best outcome for her.

I'm not a fan of the phrase "best practices." *Best* is a relative term. The "best practice" for Megan may be drastically different than what's best for you. If you're an introvert with a flair for compelling copywriting and a love of technical tools, you may have thoroughly enjoyed writing email sequences and have seen better results. There are plenty of ways to get from one place to another. What matters is finding the best way *for you*.

Let's say you want to go to a restaurant you've never been to before. You need to know how to get there, so you open your favorite map app and look up the destination. When you do, you'll see options. Do you want to walk, bike, drive, or take the bus? Avoid tolls and traffic?

Take the most fuel-efficient route? Based on your preferences, you can choose many different ways to get to the same place. And, notably for this metaphor, each path will feel different—although the final destination remains the same.

Your job works the same way. Your destination is the task or goal you need to achieve. The route you take to get there is up to you. Of course your boss plays a role, but even if you have the most micro of micromanagers, you have more control than you might think. We'll cover how to get your boss aligned shortly. For now, let's keep focused on you.

The core problem with enjoying work more is that we usually don't know our own best path. Rather, we default to the "best practices" of what everyone else is doing because... Well, that's what everyone else is doing. We follow the well-worn route many others have traveled because it seemed to work out for them.

Again, learning to enjoy your work more isn't about changing your work; it's about changing *how* you go about your work. When you do more of what you love and less of what you hate while at work, you will love your job. That's an obvious statement. Less obvious is that you're being held back because you don't know enough about your own "best path."

How well do you know you?

Think you know yourself really well? Let's see. Grab a pen, paper, and timer, then do this short exercise:

1. Start a two-minute timer.
2. Write down ten things your smartphone is great at.
3. Stop writing at ten items or when the timer ends.
4. Start the two-minute timer again.
5. Write down ten things you're great at.
6. Stop writing at ten items or when the timer ends.

How much easier was it to write your first list than your second? If you're anything like me, you breezed through the smartphone list and felt stalled on your personal list. Isn't it odd that we instantly know more about our phone's capabilities than our own? How are you going to keep aligned with your own best practices if you don't even know yourself better than your phone? I promise you'll have a much easier time with the second list pretty soon.

If you're going to find and keep on a path that makes you happier at work, you're going to need something to help you find your way. Unfortunately, Google Maps for your career hasn't been invented yet. In the days before smartphones, if you didn't have a map, you used a compass to keep you going in the right direction. To discover your optimal professional path, you need a career compass.

How to create your career compass

A career compass reorients you toward how to enjoy your job every day. When you have a task to complete, each of the four points of the compass will show you how to get your job done in a way you'll both enjoy and excel at. When you can apply at least one of the points, you're in good shape. Two will feel great. Three will feel even better. And employing all four will reward you with maximum enjoyment on the job. Here are the four points of your career compass:

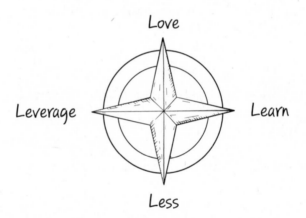

- **Love**: The more you do what you love, the better it will be for you personally and professionally.
- **Leverage**: The more you use skills you're already great at, the better you'll do and feel.
- **Learn**: The more you improve skills you care about, the more you'll enjoy your job, and the better you'll get at it too.
- **Less**: The more you avoid what you don't love doing, aren't great at, and have no interest in improving, the better you'll feel.

Perhaps you're thinking that this sounds good in theory, but you have important objectives to hit and plans to execute. You can't just change those so you get to feel better every day. Remember, your goal isn't to change what you need to do, just *how* you choose to do it. Keep the same plans and tasks you've been assigned, but choose the best path *for you* to make them happen.

For a career compass to be applicable to your day-to-day tasks, you'll need to customize the four cardinal points so they relate to what's unique about you. To start, answer the following six questions:

1. What do you love doing?
2. What are you great at?
3. Where do you want to improve?
4. What do you not love doing?
5. What are you not great at?
6. Where do you not want to improve?

For your first draft, limit yourself to about twenty minutes to answer all six questions. Then put your draft away for a few days. Return to it with fresh eyes and reevaluate your answers to see if they're still applicable and as honest as possible. Because when you're honest with yourself, you're setting your future self up for more happiness and impact.

For a template you can use to write your own career compass, go to www.yourgrassisgreener.com/resources.

To help prompt your thinking, here's more context on each question as well as a summary of Megan's answers.

1. What do you love doing?

To figure out what you truly love doing, think about what energizes you even when it's difficult. Answering this question honestly is essential because it's hard to do what you love if you don't actually know what you love doing.

Megan answered that she loves:

- listening and figuring out how to add value for people
- meeting and connecting deeply with people
- problem-solving with others

2. What are you great at?

This isn't about what you're good at doing. What are you *great* at doing? Imagine yourself in a room full of people. What can you do that you'd feel confident putting to the test against anyone else there? Don't be bashful. Knowing your strengths is necessary so you can deploy them more tactically.

Megan wrote that she's great at:

- figuring out how to add value for people
- connecting people with each other
- rallying people toward a goal

3. What do you not love doing?

These are tasks that you do but don't enjoy. By defining what you don't love, you'll get clarity on what you hope to avoid doing at work.

Megan said she doesn't love:

- sitting behind a computer all day
- working alone for too long
- organizing existing work

4. What are you not great at?

For most of us, this list could be long, but please don't be too hard on yourself. Be honest about what you feel you're not that great at. Knowing what you don't do well allows you to seek growth in those areas or to intentionally avoid them if it's not a skill you care to improve.

Megan realized she wasn't great at:

- succinct communication
- patience
- quantitative problem-solving

5. Where do you want to improve?

You likely have a few areas in which you know you need to improve and you want to put in the effort to get better. Although personal growth is usually the good kind of hard, improving yourself is still tough. It's important to be intentional about how you want to grow so that you put effort in where it needs to go.

Megan knew she wanted to improve at:

- public speaking
- helping people feel heard
- communicating succinctly

6. Where do you not want to improve?

You can't be great at everything. You will always be forced to make trade-offs for what you truly want to excel in. So what areas do you know that you don't want to improve? Writing these down will help you feel better about saying no to the wrong improvement opportunities so you can say yes to the right ones.

Megan didn't want to improve at:

- learning new tech tools (unless they helped her authentically connect with people)
- organizational skills
- project management skills

Here's what Megan's compass looked like when she was done.

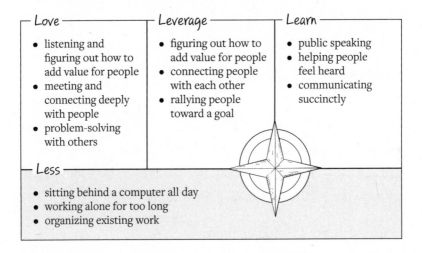

Love
- listening and figuring out how to add value for people
- meeting and connecting deeply with people
- problem-solving with others

Leverage
- figuring out how to add value for people
- connecting people with each other
- rallying people toward a goal

Learn
- public speaking
- helping people feel heard
- communicating succinctly

Less
- sitting behind a computer all day
- working alone for too long
- organizing existing work

When she saw her compass laid out like this, it was immediately clear to her why she'd wanted to unsubscribe from herself. Nothing about the email automation task aligned with what she excelled at or what gave her joy on the job. When Megan spent time considering how best to align her *how* to her *what*, she discovered an alternate path—her personal best practice. To find potential customers while not killing her joy at work, Megan used her career compass to lead her toward this solution:

- Because she **loves** connecting with people, she invited potential customers to a conference where she could meet with them in person and talk one-on-one.
- Because she wanted to **leverage** how she enjoys adding value to others, she spent time in actual conversations listening for needs she could fill.
- Because she wanted to **learn** and improve her public-speaking skills, she invited the potential customers at the conference to a meeting where she gave a presentation.
- And because she wanted much **less** time sitting behind a computer all day, she threw it out of the window. (Again, actually, that's what I would have done.) Rather, she found ways to sit less and engage more with others throughout her day.

Megan discovered a way to hit the goal she had been given in her own best way. With the clarity of her career compass, she rethought how she was working and found an approach that hit all four cardinal points—doing something she loved, leveraging a skill she already had, learning a skill she wanted to develop, and doing less of what she knew she didn't enjoy.

How you're working might be the only hurdle to enjoying your job more. Your dream job isn't a position you get one day; it's a job you practice every day. The key is to consistently practice your own best ways of working.

How to bring your boss along for the ride

"What about my manager?"

That's the most common question I hear as people implement their career compass. Of course, you cannot ignore your boss and do whatever you want all the time. But I believe you have more control over how you work than you think. Too often, we assume we have to work a certain way and never simply try or even ask to try a different approach. If your boss is so brutal that you feel you could lose your job just for asking, it might be a sign that you're in a toxic environment and should consider leaving.

In most cases, however, even a mediocre manager will give you at least some leeway to decide how to get your job done. Other times, even a fantastic boss might need you to work in ways that are completely out of your control. In either case, what's important is that you try to do every task in the best way for you. It's better to make an attempt to align your manager on the approach you want to take than to assume you can't and never try.

Whether you think you have control over how you work or not, start from the position of assuming that you do. I think you'll be surprised at the results when you try. For any given task, use your compass to figure out the best *how* for you. Once you're clear on the approach you'd like to take, you can work to align your manager. If they support you, you're off to the races. If not, at least you'll know for sure that you need to go another route. If your manager does turn you down, going through the motions will help you learn how to better align them for future work.

Here's an approach you can use with your boss:

1. Use your compass to come up with the best path for you.

2. Ask your boss: "Can I decide how I get this done?" (Recall the first step in decision-making from Chapter 2, "Who is making this decision?")

3. If you own the decision of how to do the work, take a moment to inform your manager of your plan, then get to work.

4. If you do not get to decide, ask them: "What would need to be true for me to do it like this [insert your desired approach]?" Focus the discussion on what *would* be needed and not on all of the reasons you don't get to do it your way.

5. Thank them for having the conversation with you. (Either way, a little gratitude goes a long way.)

If you have a good manager, they'll appreciate the thought you put into how you work. They may also have helpful input to improve the path you're planning to take. If your manager turns you down, remember to ask them why. Sometimes the nature of your work or the specifics of your situation will mean your boss has to say no. If you find that you're hearing no a lot and want more control over how you do your job, it may be time to share feedback with your manager. We'll cover how to do that in Chapter 8. For now, start using your compass and having conversations with your manager to see if you can discover more work joy right where you are.

The next most common question I hear is, "How do I keep on track?"

Keeping on your path

Be present. Stay in the moment. There's a reason for these sayings. Studies show that you're happiest (and most effective) when you're focused on the here and now. But there's clear evidence that we spend nearly half our time thinking about something other than the task at hand, and this mind wandering makes you feel less happy. Also, recall hedonic adaptation, the tendency for your happiness to fade after accomplishing a milestone. Your happiness is measured in your moments.

Though you likely know what sayings like *be in the moment* mean, figuring out how to apply them is much harder. Between all of the goals, meetings, decisions, and pressures at the office, it's almost as if work environments are purpose-built to pull you off your best practices and out of the present moment. Did you do well on that last project? Are you working on the right tasks right now? Will you be successful this year?

You can use your compass to help you stay in the moment. Anytime you get a new task, use your compass to figure out how to make it happen. When you find yourself getting distracted away from your day-to-day work—stressing about milestones, worrying that you're doing things differently than everyone else around you, or simply disliking what you're doing—you can again turn to your compass and let it guide you back to the best way to work for you. Your compass keeps you in the moment. But how do you know your compass is right?

Your manager can be a big help for you here as well. (Aren't they great?) Ask your manager for an hour-long review meeting roughly every three months. Don't wait for them to book reviews with you. This isn't about a yearly check-in on your salary or whether you're getting promoted. Use a quarterly meeting to intentionally get out of your day-to-day. Look back at what you've accomplished, and ahead at what you plan to do next. This will help you make sure that your compass is aligned with where you need to go. When you know your compass is aligned, you'll question it less and can be more confident following it for your daily tasks.

I find it's best if you and your manager both prepare your thinking in advance of a regular review. That way you can use the time you spend together for a deeper discussion. Here are a few questions to help guide your preparation:

Ask yourself:

- How is work feeling for you?
- How do you feel you are performing?

Ask your manager:

- How does your manager feel you are performing?
- What could you do differently to enjoy your job and have more impact going forward?

Having an open discussion with your manager will help you identify any changes you might need to make to your compass. Some companies use professional development plans and a regular review process to capture this concept. If that's what your company does, you can use your compass as the foundation for a more specific professional development plan. If you're not sure how to write a professional development plan (or don't enjoy the process), you can go to www.yourgrassisgreener.com/resources for a step-by-step guide on how to use your career compass and AI to automatically create a custom-tailored professional development plan for you.

Your compass keeps your day-to-day on the best path for you, and regular manager reviews keep your compass pointing in the right direction for your job.

No joke

Best practices are rarely best for everyone. The key to enjoying your job more is finding ways to practice your own best approach on any given task. The more you do what you enjoy and avoid what you don't, the better your job will become. You might not enjoy every moment, nor will work always be easy, but it will be more energizing. Whether or not you already have your dream job depends on how you work, not what you work on.

Once Megan used her career compass to change her approach to the task she struggled with before, the tactic paid off. As Megan leveraged who she is and what she's best at, she experienced exponential growth in both her enjoyment and her impact. Only a few months after her initial low point, her list of prospects surpassed eight figures in potential revenue. Same task, different route—much better outcome. She was loving her work and everyone was loving her results.

While she still has moments she doesn't love, Megan's never been happier with what she's doing day-to-day. After her drastic turnaround, Megan met with her manager for a regular review.

When she shared the new results she was delivering, her smiling boss had only one thing to say: "You gotta be kidding me!"

ACTION EXERCISE

Schedule twenty minutes to start working on your career compass this week. Start by answering these questions:

1. What do you love doing?
2. What are you great at?
3. Where do you want to improve?
4. What do you not love doing?
5. What are you not great at?
6. Where do you not want to improve?

When you're done, sketch out your career compass and use it to guide how you approach the next task you're assigned.

Further reading in case you feel like it

- *So Good They Can't Ignore You*, Cal Newport—Challenges common advice to follow your passion and instead focuses on building valuable skills to achieve success.

- *The Happiness Hypothesis*, Jonathan Haidt—An interesting mixture of what ancient wisdom and modern psychology tell us about how to be happy.

- *Wherever You Go, There You Are: Mindfulness Meditation in Everyday Life*, Jon Kabat-Zinn—In this book, Jon Kabat-Zinn introduces readers to the practice of mindfulness and provides practical guidance on integrating it into daily routines.

How to Enjoy Your Day-to-Day Work More (Without Changing Jobs)

Chapter 4 **How to promote the imposter in you**

When you try to turn off imposter syndrome, you wind up feeling worse and your performance drops too. Instead, use your self-doubt as the very thing to build more confidence and a better sense that you do belong. When you feel imposter syndrome:

1. Ask follow-up questions in one-on-one meetings to learn what you don't know and build stronger relationships in the process.
2. Redirect your focus from what your team does better than you to what you can uniquely bring to them.
3. Once you feel comfortable, start asking more questions in group settings so you can help get the most out of your team.

Chapter 5 **How to measure your joy on the job**

The more you enjoy your job, the better you do at it. Despite workplaces focusing almost exclusively on measuring your milestones, it's your moments that lead to lasting joy on your job. How to measure your moments:

1. On the left side of a piece of paper, write a list of what you enjoy doing.

2.   On the right side of the page, write a list of everything you actually spent your time doing over the past week (reference your calendar).

3.   How much time did you spend doing what you enjoy?

Chapter 6 **How to unlock more joy at your job**

You don't get a dream job, you practice it. The challenge is that best practices for one person are rarely best practices for you. Pressures and priorities make it hard for you to work in your own best way.

Before you start a task, use your career compass to guide your best approach to any task: doing something you love, leveraging an existing skill, learning a new one, and doing less of what you don't enjoy doing. Answer these questions to create your compass:

- What do you love doing?
- What are you great at?
- Where do you want to improve?
- What do you not love doing?
- What are you not great at?
- Where do you not want to improve?

PART 3

How to Progress Faster
(Without Waiting for a Promotion)

You've freed up your time and found new ways to enjoy your day-to-day work more. What's next? Your progression.

A big part of caring about your career is feeling like you're improving. Unfortunately, the conventional view on career progression is too narrow, limiting the advancement you're truly capable of. More often than not, progress gets simplified down to achieving milestones like promotions and new job titles.

By now you know that measuring your milestones is not the way. When you rely on achievement alone, you also give up control of your progress. Promotions need approvals, and job titles have to be available for you.

True advancement is about improving yourself—which is completely in your control. I don't mean sitting in a cave meditating. I mean developing the specific skills that will open more doors to more opportunities for you.

UNLEASH

No more waiting for an annual review or for your boss to decide you're ready. In Part 3, we'll focus on specific tactics you can use to accelerate your own advancement and level up any team you're on.

Implementing the tactics from the following three chapters will unleash the next level of your growth. You'll feel great looking back at the progress you'll make, and it won't be long before your boss notices as well. Each chapter to follow will focus on a key insight you're overlooking:

- **Chapter 7:** Better decisions unlock better outcomes—you're missing the best way to decide.
- **Chapter 8:** More feedback unlocks faster growth—you're not getting enough feedback.
- **Chapter 9:** Opportunities to outperform are everywhere— you (and everyone else) are missing them.

When I point out what you've been missing, the gaps will feel obvious. You won't be surprised. But you will be surprised when you see the results you get from applying these solutions.

We'll start with a simple question: Have you heard of my friend Paul?

THE WORLD'S BEST SOCCER PROPHET

How to Make Better Decisions

The first principle is that you must not fool yourself, and you are the easiest person to fool.

—RICHARD FEYNMAN

Paul was born in the seaside town of Weymouth, England. As a baby he moved to Germany, growing up and living the rest of his life in the city of Oberhausen. From a young age, it was clear that Paul had a gift for swimming. Although he was a natural in the water, able to swim before he could walk, his true passion was soccer. Despite his love of the sport, Paul's athletic prowess in the pool didn't translate to the pitch. His playing style was often described as "a mess of tangled legs." Perhaps realizing that he'd always come up short as a player, Paul redirected his passion from playing to analysis—and that's how he became famous.

Paul first garnered local notice when he successfully predicted the outcome of four of Germany's six European Championship matches, outperforming much more seasoned analysts. His fame went global when he posted a perfect record in predicting the winner of all of Germany's 2010 World Cup matches, including a German win over heavily favored Uruguay. The odds of anyone else predicting results as well as Paul is about 0.56 percent. In fact, if you'd bet $150 on Paul's choices that year, you would have won

$64,500. Looking to go out at the top of his game, Paul retired after the 2010 season. He finished his career with an impressive 86 percent prediction accuracy, nearly double what leading sports analysts and artificial intelligence systems can accomplish today, almost fifteen years later.

If you want to make better decisions at work and in life, you should follow Paul's strategy. Obviously, he had an incredible method of analyzing players' strengths and weaknesses, while factoring in variables like the weather and how other analysts were sizing up the match. His decisions ultimately revealed a stunning intellect that could apparently see into the future with remarkable clarity and foresight. How helpful would that kind of intuition be in solving the issues you're facing right now?

There's just one problem: Paul was an octopus. At the Sea Life Centre in Oberhausen, his keepers would set two boxes in front of him, each bearing the respective flags of the competing teams. The same tasty treat would be placed in each box. (Paul was apparently partial to mussels and oysters.) If Paul ate from the box with the German flag, then he was "choosing" Germany to win that match. Paul became known as the Octopus Oracle, and millions of people around the world watched his match predictions.

So the quick and easy solution to making better decisions at work and in life is to buy an octopus. I'm kidding, but here's the real reason I wanted you to know about Paul: great decision-making isn't about the outcome. It's about your approach.

Yes, Paul had astounding results, but it's hard to argue that his decision-making was any good. If you were standing on the edge of a cliff and Paul had boxes marked *Jump* and *Don't Jump*, would you let him make that decision for you? Would you trust him with any decisions at all? Paul just happened to get lucky. Statistically speaking, if you put about 180 octopi in a room, you'd almost certainly get one with the same prediction performance as Paul (how you get them all in there is up to you).

No matter how hard you try, you will never fully control the outcome of your decisions. In fact, the only aspect of the decision-making process you have complete control over is how you make your decisions themselves. Sometimes you'll make great decisions and everything will work out. Other times, they won't. There's always an element of chance. That's why the hallmark of great decision-making is how you decide, not just what happens afterward. When you improve your approach to making decisions, you maximize the chances of getting the outcomes you want.

In this chapter, I'm going to show you a three-step method for making better decisions. When you use it, you'll get stuck less often on tough choices and feel more confident about your decisions— even if things go wrong later. Most importantly, better decision-making will increase your chances of getting the results you want from your choices. Improving your decision-making today inherently improves every future decision you will face. Given how many decisions you make every day, even small improvements have the potential to significantly impact your life overall.

At work, the more often you make better decisions, the more you'll be recognized and sought out for important projects, and the faster you'll progress as a result. If becoming a manager is interesting to you, decision-making is even more important. Management is, essentially, the art of great decision-making. If you want to excel in work and in life, making better decisions is essential.

So why are decisions as challenging for us as it was for Paul to play soccer? Why do our brains often feel like "a mess of tangled legs" when it comes to the choices we struggle with?

Your brain is lazy

Because your brain *is* a mess of tangled legs, or at least a mess of 100 billion neurons and their 25 quadrillion pathways. With so many routes to take, your brain evolved to find the fastest, easiest way to make decisions. It does this because decision-making takes a lot of thinking, and thinking takes a lot of energy. Though it accounts for just 2 percent of your body weight, your brain uses 20 percent of your energy. Brains are great, but they're costly. For most of human existence, food wasn't easy to find, so our brains evolved for efficiency. To make decisions as easily as possible, your brain evolved to be lazy.

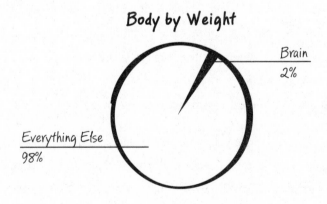

Body by Weight

Brain
2%

Everything Else
98%

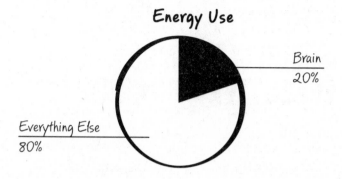

The size of your brain compared to how much energy it uses.

No matter how lazy, brains still had to make decisions or they'd wind up as some lion's lunch, along with the other 98 percent of the body. That's why your brain developed mental shortcuts. When faced with decisions, your brain has a number of unseen ways of helping you get to an answer quickly (and cheaply) without doing the necessary deep thinking. That's perfect for spotting a hungry lion out of the corner of your eye and moving your legs before you've had a chance to think. But it's much less helpful for the rational analyses you need to make great decisions today.

The problem is that efficient thinking is rarely the most effective thinking. Anytime you're making a decision, your brain is finding ways to skip the hard work. What's worse is that you're unaware it's even happening. For example, in the amount of time we need to blink our eyes—about 33 milliseconds—we make lasting judgments about a person's character just by looking at their faces. Instead of judging people on their character, which requires time and effort, we routinely judge them on their appearance, which is faster and easier. We don't do this because we're all superficial. We do it because our brains are simply wired that way.

EFFICIENT THINKING IS RARELY THE MOST **EFFECTIVE** THINKING.

Behind the scenes, your brain is programmed to swap hard questions for easier ones and offer up answers as if the two different questions were the same. Take elections, for example. Deciding who to vote for is hard. You probably feel like you think deeply about the issues in order to make an informed choice. Turns out, however, that five-year-old children can accurately predict election outcomes in foreign countries—with languages they can't understand—by looking only at pictures of the candidates and picking the one they think looks best. Either five-year-olds are all as lucky as Paul, or voting adults are deciding based on appearance more than they know. You want to decide who you think the best candidate is, but your brain tells you who looks better instead.

These mental shortcuts are known as *unconscious biases* because you can't know when they are happening to you. That's what makes quality decision-making so hard. You're being poorly influenced by your own biology, and you don't suspect a thing. Over 180 different biases have been identified to date, including:

- **Groupthink:** deciding based on popular opinion rather than deep analysis (Chapter 2).
- **Planning fallacy:** deciding how long a task will take based on how long you want it to take rather than data about how long similar tasks have taken in the past (Chapter 3).

- **Confirmation bias:** deciding based on what you already believe rather than a fair assessment of the information available (Chapter 9).

Your decision-making may feel rational, but you can't outrun thousands of years of evolution. Your neurons will always fire faster than your rational analysis.

You can't eliminate biases from your thinking entirely, but you can take different approaches to lessen their effects. What you need is a way to step back and force your brain to do something it doesn't want to do—think deeply about your decisions. So how can you make better decisions when even your own brain is working against you?

A Nobel Prize in how to decide

Daniel was born on March 5, 1934. He grew up in Israel before moving to the United States for university. He's an average swimmer and soccer player—and definitely not an octopus. His full name is Daniel Kahneman and he is one of the psychologists credited with discovering unconscious biases. In 2002 he won a Nobel Prize for his work in exploring human decision-making. So we may want to listen to him more than to our friend Paul.

Throughout his career, Kahneman has shown that you can reduce the impact of unconscious biases by changing your approach to thinking and making decisions. In 1956, when Kahneman was twenty-one, he was tasked with finding a way to evaluate potential soldiers as candidates for combat duty. Until that point, soldiers were selected by an interviewer's holistic decision: Do you think this person will make a great soldier? That is a hard question to answer based on an interview, and by now you know what your brain does with hard questions.

Kahneman knew this too, so he came up with a different approach. He didn't ask interviewers to make the final decision. Instead, he provided standard questions designed to evaluate each candidate on relevant traits and had the interviewers score them on each one. Trait scores were then combined to algorithmically determine whether or not to select a candidate. Frustrated at being reduced to an algorithm, the interviewers pushed back. Like most people, they believed their intuitions were very accurate. So, to satisfy their egos, Kahneman asked them to close their eyes after each interview, imagine the candidate as a combat soldier, and provide a final, holistic score from zero to ten.

Before Kahneman's method, there was no correlation between an interviewer's assessments and the candidate's future combat performance. Kahneman's algorithmic approach was much more predictive. More surprisingly, the interviewers' holistic assessments—which were previously useless before they had to think through the trait scores Kahneman gave them—were now just as predictive of success as the algorithm itself.

Asking the right questions can force your brain to do the right thinking. When you start by evaluating the factors of a decision, you become primed to think more analytically. It's this initial priming that improves your overall decision-making. By creating a predetermined routine for your thinking, as Kahneman did for soldier selection, you can consistently reduce the impact of your biases and make decisions that are the most effective, even if they aren't the most efficient.

The idea of a thought routine might feel new, but you already routinely use routines. When you come home and put your keys in the same place you always do, that's a routine to help you find them in the morning. You likely already use thought routines too, though you may not know it by that phrase. When was the last time you were faced with a decision and wrote out a pros and cons list to help you decide? Listing pros and cons is a thought routine, probably the most popular one, but it's not very good.

Why you should upgrade from pros and cons

It's been many decades since Kahneman showed us a better decision-making routine, and yet we continue to use bad ones. Don't beat yourself up, though. Biases get in the way of even the most seasoned executives too, like Bob Iger. He was the CEO of Disney from 2005 to 2020 and has since returned for a second tenure.

During his first fifteen years, Iger was widely regarded as one of the most successful media executives of that time. Within his first two years on the job, Iger oversaw Disney's purchase of Pixar for $7.4 billion. The acquisition went on to become one of the most successful deals in Disney's history. In his book *The Ride of a Lifetime*, Bob shares how pros and cons almost resulted in a decision not to pursue the deal at all.

Steve Jobs was Pixar's CEO at the time, and Iger called him up to pitch the idea. Jobs agreed to meet in person and Iger flew to Apple's headquarters to discuss the deal. It went how many of your meetings probably go, except with more turtlenecks. Jobs stood at the whiteboard while they brainstormed a list of pros and cons.

Iger let Jobs lead, and Jobs promptly and bluntly wrote, "Disney's culture will destroy Pixar!" Iger says he couldn't blame Jobs for that statement. Jobs continued with his cons until writing in all caps: "DISTRACTION WILL KILL PIXAR'S CREATIVITY." Jobs' list was so long that Iger chose not to add any cons of his own and moved them on to discuss the pros.

This time, Iger led the discussion and opened with a very Disneyfied answer: "Disney will be saved by Pixar and we'll all live happily ever after." Their conversation lasted for another two hours. As Iger writes, "The pros were meager and the cons were abundant."

When faced with so many obvious issues and so few potential benefits, it's hard to argue against the black-and-white nature of a pros and cons list. Iger let his disappointment be known and said, "It was a nice idea. But I don't see how we do this."

Obviously I wasn't there, but I can almost see Jobs smiling at the whiteboard, thinking differently about the list. In reply—and in the face of apparent evidence to the contrary—Steve Jobs gave a very Jobsian answer: "A few solid pros are more powerful than dozens of cons."

> ## A few solid pros are more powerful than dozens of cons.
> —**Steve Jobs**

Jobs was highlighting Iger's flawed thought routine. The Disney CEO was looking at the pros and cons and deciding based on which list had more items. The decision to purchase Pixar was incredibly complicated and involved a lot of interrelated data, billions of dollars, public investment markets, and so much more to take into account. In other words, the choice was both hard and slow, which our brains can't stand. So unconsciously, Iger's brain opted for the faster, more efficient routine: comparing the number of pros and cons.

But as Jobs pointed out, the number of pros and cons doesn't matter. It's the relative strength of each one that should be the deciding factor. Where Iger's brain unknowingly simplified the problem down to comparing the size of the lists, Jobs forced their thinking through each item. Like Kahneman's interviewers, their decision-making was better as a result.

Disney bought Pixar and, in less than ten years, Pixar's films earned over $15 billion worldwide, averaging more than $500 million per film. Disney did not destroy Pixar's culture, nor did distraction kill their creativity. Great execution obviously helped turn their great decision into a very positive (and lucrative) outcome for both companies. But what's more interesting to me, and more applicable to you, is the way the decision was made. The next time you're tempted to make a decision with a pros and cons list, remember Bob and Steve and opt for a better routine.

Use factors to make better decisions

Instead of listing pros and cons, list *factors*. A factor doesn't tell you which option is better; it tells you how to think about which option is better. For instance, culture would be the factor for Jobs' con: "Disney's culture will destroy Pixar!" Listing factors will help you think through the important aspects of your decisions while priming your decision-making to be more analytical, like Kahneman's research showed us.

Once you've listed the relevant factors to any decision, you can then use a simple but effective thought routine to make your choice. It's based on combining Kahneman's and Jobs' methods, but you don't need to be a Nobel Prize winner or tech genius to use it. Nor do you need to wear a turtleneck, but if that helps you think better, then by all means, wear one. I've used the following routine to make hundreds of my own decisions, and I've helped my clients make hundreds more of their own decisions with it as well. You can use it for any decision, big or small. When you feel stuck, not knowing what to decide, it will help unstick you. And it will prime you to be more analytical—decreasing the impact of biases and increasing the quality of your decisions.

The factors thought routine has three steps:

1. List every relevant factor in your decision.
2. Make a mini-decision based on each factor alone.
3. Make a final decision considering all of the factors together.

This routine works because it helps you avoid the mental shortcuts that hurt your decision-making. By listing the relevant factors first, you avoid letting less important information sway your opinion—like how many pros or cons there are. Then, the routine forces you to think deeply about what decision you would make considering each factor as if it were the only one. Having that thinking done before you holistically consider all factors together will make your final decision better.

Because few of us are likely to make $7.4 billion acquisitions anytime soon, let's use a much simpler, more relatable example: what to eat for lunch. (In retrospect, this might have helped Katharine avoid food poisoning.)

STEP 1: List every relevant factor in your decision

Let's say you are deciding between getting sushi or a submarine sandwich for lunch. The relevant factors could be:

- **Health:** Which choice is better for you?
- **Cost:** Which choice is the cheapest?
- **Speed:** Which choice will you be eating soonest?
- **Quantity:** Which choice is going to fill you up more?
- **Gut feeling:** What feels right in the moment?

With each factor listed, move on to Step 2.

STEP 2: Make a mini-decision based on each factor alone

Next, figure out what you would decide if you were making your decision based on each factor alone, as if none of the other factors existed.

- If all you cared about was **health**: Pick sushi. Raw fish is good for you.
- If all you cared about was **cost**: Pick the sub. It's cheaper.
- If all you cared about was **speed**: Pick the sub. It's close and ready in minutes.
- If all you cared about was **quantity**: Pick the sub. All that bread is filling. (Heads up for the late-afternoon carb crash, though.)
- If all you cared about was your **gut feeling**: Pick sushi. It just feels right.

Remember, the goal here is not to count up the overall score. That's the unconscious bias that Bob Iger almost fell for, which is why there's one more step in the routine.

STEP 3: Make a final decision considering all of the factors together

At this point, your shortcut-minded brain may be thinking, *Why can't I just count up which option had more "votes?" Wouldn't that save me time and effort?*

It certainly would, but it would also be a worse decision. Step 1 listed the factors that are important to your decision. This makes it clear, in advance, how you're going to make the decision so you don't get swayed by irrelevant information later. *More votes* was not a factor, therefore it's not relevant to your decision. The purpose of Step 2 wasn't to tally scores, but rather to force your thinking to consider each important factor before jumping to a conclusion. The act of doing that thinking, regardless of what you decide, is what makes your decision better.

Perhaps, having thought through the factors, you really want sushi. Or maybe that foot-long sub is calling your name. Whatever you ultimately decide to have for lunch is up to you. Just don't decide until after you've considered the context of each factor alone.

This was obviously a trivial example, but you can use the thought routine for any decision. If you're deciding whether or not to hire a candidate, you could consider technical ability, communication, adaptability, and cultural fit factors. For a new product direction, the factors might be time to market, revenue potential, amount of work, and probability of success. The point of the example isn't the decision you make, but rather, how you make the decision.

The factors routine prevents you from taking the mental shortcuts your brain craves, ultimately leading to better decisions. You now have the core of the routine, and here are two quick tips to help you deploy it for even better results.

Use your emotions to make better decisions

Conventional wisdom holds that important decisions should be made rationally and with little to no consideration for feelings. But emotions always play a part in your thinking, and to deny them any say in your decision-making is to deny a significant influence on the process. In his book *Descartes' Error,* Antonio Damasio, a prominent neuroscientist, tells the story of an emotionless patient named

Elliot. During brain surgery to remove a tumor, Elliot lost much of his ventromedial prefrontal cortex, the part of the brain integral to processing emotions.

After recovering from the surgery, tests showed that his IQ, memory, learning, language, and other capacities were fine. But when Elliot was tested for emotional responses, he felt nothing. His intellect was intact, but his emotions were gone. The ramifications of his situation came to light anytime he had to make decisions. For example, when deciding how to organize research papers at work, he deliberated on the best approach for hours. By date? Size? Relevance? Ultimately, he couldn't make a single decision. Elliot's inability to feel emotions stymied his decision-making, even for something as seemingly simple as paperwork organization.

While emotions shouldn't lead your decisions, you still need them to make a decision. If you're feeling really strong emotions, it's probably not the best time to decide. Take time to cool off and come back to the decision when you're feeling more under control. Once you do, you'll want to factor in whatever your gut feeling is telling you. The best way to do that is simply by adding "gut feel" as a factor and treating it like any other in your routine.

Your gut might make you feel like today is a sushi day. No need to explore the feeling further. Just write it down and consider it as a factor before stepping back to think about all of the factors together to make your final decision.

WHILE EMOTIONS SHOULDN'T LEAD YOUR DECISIONS, YOU STILL **NEED** THEM TO MAKE A DECISION.

Get thinking out of your head

Using a routine helps provide structure to your thinking. When decisions are more challenging than what to eat for lunch, there's a lot more context to consider. By getting thinking out of your head and onto a page (paper or digital), you will be better able to see and assess any gaps in your analysis. In Chapter 2 we covered how your decisions will get even better when you involve other people. When you write down how you're thinking about a decision, you can show it to your colleagues, which makes it easier for them to contribute. After all, they can't help you see what you might be missing if they don't know what you've already considered.

To help you collect your thinking and make your own decisions using the factors routine, you can get a free copy of the framework I use with my clients from my book website at www.yourgrassisgreener. com/resources. The framework gives you a step-by-step approach for making any decision a great one.

Here's a brief rundown of what the framework covers:

- **Decision to be made:** One sentence that clearly articulates the decision being made. It's hard to make a decision if you're not even clear what the decision actually is.

- **Who is making the decision?** The name of the person or people making the decision. Decisions don't make themselves (see Chapter 2).

- **When will the decision get made?** The specific date by which you're going to decide. This increases the likelihood that the decision gets made on time (see Chapter 2).

- **How hard will it be to change the decision later?** If it's relatively easy to change your mind later, you can make the decision much more quickly than if it's hard to change later.

- **Relevant context to consider:** Show yourself and others what information is being considered to help make sure you have what you need to decide well.

- **Factors routine:** Unless you've skipped right to the end of this chapter, you know what this is. Make sure you use it.

- **Confidence in the proposed decision:** A percentage assessment of your confidence in the proposed decision. Low confidence means you need to do more work, high confidence means you're ready to decide. I usually find anything above 50 percent is fine for easy-to-change decisions and 75 percent or more for harder-to-change decisions.

- **Other options considered and why not to go with them:** Use a bullet point for each option with a sentence or two on why it isn't being selected. This ensures that you've considered your options, and summarizing why you're not choosing them will help you avoid confirmation bias.

Using a framework to write your decisions down is the final tip to prevent your mind from taking unhelpful shortcuts so you can arrive at better decisions.

Use a routine, not an octopus

Making decisions is hard because your brain is working against you. Human brains evolved to take mental shortcuts that, though highly efficient, are less than effective in today's workplace. Worse yet, your brain is feeding you bad information all the time—without you even knowing it! You can't avoid unconscious biases altogether, but you can reduce their impact. You also can't completely control exactly what happens after you make a decision, but you can improve your odds of getting the outcomes you want.

The key is using a thought routine—a predetermined path for your thinking—to force your brain to consider the factors that matter most. But not all routines are created equal. Using a pros and cons list, though highly popular, is not the best approach. Instead, learn from Daniel Kahneman and Steve Jobs. When faced with a decision, use the factors routine to make it better:

1. List every relevant factor in your decision.
2. Make a mini-decision based on each factor alone.
3. Make a final decision considering all of the factors together.

Big or small, following the factors routine will improve every decision you need to make. So the next time you're out for sushi, factor in Paul and consider skipping the octopus.

Perhaps in return, he'll decide not to have you jump off that cliff!

For the next important decision you need to make:

1. Use the factors routine to propose a decision.

2. Include your gut feeling as one of the factors to consider.

3. Capture your thinking in a framework.

4. Show the framework to at least one other person and ask, "What am I missing?"

5. Make the decision and get moving.

Once you've done this, reflect on what you learned:

- How would you rate the quality of the decision?
- What helped? What didn't? How might you improve the next decision?

Further reading in case you feel like it

- *Thinking, Fast and Slow*, Daniel Kahneman—The preeminent book on unconscious biases from one of the founders of the field. It's a bit dense, but the details are often worth it.

- *Descartes' Error*, Antonio Damasio—A deep dive into the role of your emotions in rational thinking.

- *Thinking in Bets*, Annie Duke—A book written by a professional poker player turned author focused on cognitive-behavioral decision-making. What could be better?

YOU BOUGHT HOW MUCH TOILET PAPER?

How to Get More Feedback

Average players want to be left alone. Good players want to be coached. Great players want to be told the truth.

—DOC RIVERS

Cam is one of the best executive coaches I have ever met. Prior to private practice, Cam was hired as the founding member of Shopify's Talent Acceleration Team. His mandate was to grow the capabilities of Shopify's employees as fast as the company itself was growing. And growth was blazingly fast. Even in their early days, Shopify quickly began eating into Amazon's ecommerce dominance. Shopify's platform powers the online sales of millions of merchants and is approaching $1 trillion USD in total sales.

Ask Cam about his experience, however, and he'll tell you it wasn't always up and to the right. I wanted to learn more about how Shopify helped employees progress so quickly and Cam told me a story about a failed project and the resulting honest feedback he got from his boss, Shopify's CEO. The feedback was so honest that, even all these years later, Cam still vividly remembers walking out of that particular meeting feeling like a new orifice had been ripped into the lower half of his body (paraphrasing for politeness).

Early in his tenure, Cam and a colleague developed a multiday course to teach employees skills for exponential growth. On a snowy winter's day in Canada, he pulled every employee from their Toronto office into a day-long training offsite. As they began, he wanted the team to focus on what was being taught, so he asked everyone to put away their devices. Sounds innocent enough, right?

However, he'd forgotten to inform anyone at the C-level. Sure enough, an executive unknowingly walked into the office that day with an urgent request, only to find it was completely empty. Not a single person appeared to be at work. Confused, they started emailing, instant messaging, and calling around to figure out what was going on. This, of course, didn't work because everyone was diligently following Cam's instructions to keep off their devices. The training ended and the urgent need passed unmet. Bad for Cam. Worse when his boss found out and shared some especially juicy feedback with him.

Tough feedback is hard to hear, but it's always better to hear it than not. When you know about it, you can do something about it. Ignorance might be bliss, but it won't make you any better. Smartly, Cam listened to his boss's feedback and set out to change his tactics as a result. He realized that lengthy office-wide training sessions were not going to work, so he began paring the program down into its single most essential element.

Despite the challenging feedback he received, Cam knew that free-flowing feedback was critical to achieving the incredible growth Shopify had planned. Research has shown that more feedback helps you learn and develop new skills faster, improves what you're able to achieve, and increases your overall motivation as well. It's also been shown that teams with free-flowing feedback significantly outperform those without. That's why Cam set out to find a way to increase feedback and cement it as a regular habit in Shopify's culture.

IF YOU CARE ABOUT YOUR OWN DEVELOPMENT, FOCUS ON THE **QUALITY AND QUANTITY OF FEEDBACK YOU GET.**

Can you remember the last time you were told something painful that ultimately helped you improve? How often do you hear really helpful feedback in general? If you're like most people, you don't get enough feedback, and even if you do, more is always better. That means you either have, will have, or are currently facing a similar challenge to Cam's: how to get more feedback flowing.

Getting feedback is hard

As conclusive as the evidence is that feedback supercharges people's growth, it's equally clear that most of us aren't getting enough. Too little feedback can easily be holding you back from progressing in your career. Perhaps you meet with your manager a few times a year, or get the occasional comment from a colleague, but that isn't usually enough to make meaningful change. To understand why you're not getting more feedback, all you have to do is look in the mirror.

Have you ever wanted to give someone helpful feedback but ultimately decided not to? Every excuse comes to mind:

- They'll get offended.
- They won't like me anymore.
- I don't know how to say what I want to say.
- They don't want to hear from me.
- I don't know how it will turn out.

Giving feedback comes with social risks, and because we're unsure how someone may take our feedback, we often decide to play it safe and keep it to ourselves. The reason you don't get enough feedback from your colleagues is because, just like you, they don't give enough feedback either. Like the empty shelves in the toilet paper aisle after a spree of pandemic panic-buying, feedback is in short supply. There simply isn't enough of it being shared to go around.

Studies show that feedback is in short supply because we overestimate the risks of giving feedback while underestimating the benefits it would provide. Researchers from Harvard also found that we share only about half of the feedback we have because of how often we assume (wrongly) that other people don't want to hear it from us—further increasing the supply shortage. Everyone wants more feedback, but very few are willing to provide it. To fix a supply shortage, all you have to do is increase the supply. Luckily, you're in a perfect position to do just that.

You can be the change you want to see in your workplace by taking the first, sometimes scary step of giving more feedback to others. The more feedback you give your colleagues, the more of it you will get for yourself. I'll show you why that is, how to make it easier for you to give feedback to others, and how to make it easier for them to give more feedback to you. By the end of this chapter, you'll have everything Cam was searching for: a way to unleash the unparalleled growth potential of feedback.

Giving is getting

If there's a lack in the amount of feedback you get, you need to increase the amount *you give*. The secret superpower of feedback is that the more you give it, the more you get it back. A particularly helpful characteristic of human nature explains why. Reciprocity bias is yet another of your many unconscious biases. It describes your subconscious desire to return favors.

THE MORE FEEDBACK YOU **GIVE**, THE MORE FEEDBACK YOU **GET**.

The theory behind reciprocity bias is that our ancestors learned to share their food and skills with one another because their survival depended on it. Fast-forward a few millennia and this is why many restaurants offer mints with your bill. According to a study by the *Journal of Applied Social Psychology*, offering candy with a bill increases tips by over 20 percent. Why? Because when you receive a mint, you subconsciously feel obligated to reciprocate. Since you're staring at the bill, you repay your minty fresh breath with a better tip.

Although reciprocity bias can be used against you in predatory sales practices, when employed purposefully and positively, the bias can create a win-win scenario for everyone. As you give feedback, you'll get feedback. As you get feedback, you'll give feedback. It's a virtuous cycle that everyone benefits from.

Virtuous Feedback Cycle

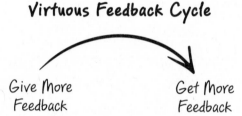

Give More
Feedback

Get More
Feedback

Now, to be clear, I'm not advocating that you offer someone a piece of your mind and then stand there staring at them until they return the favor. Rather, you should consistently offer genuine feedback on a day-to-day basis. As you do so, you are steadily increasing other people's feelings of wanting to reciprocate and provide useful feedback to you as well. Eventually, that's exactly what will happen. Your supply shortage will turn into a surplus.

But giving more feedback is *hard*.

How to give more feedback

We don't offer feedback as often as we should due to fear: fear of hurt feelings, fear of the unknown, fear of being misunderstood, etc. There's always a risk that what you say won't land well, and that's why the way you share feedback is important. Structured well, you can significantly reduce the risk of your conversations going off the rails.

Give better feedback

To keep your feedback in a safe zone, steer clear of right and wrong. Don't get into a situation where your comments can be perceived as correct or incorrect, because that's where arguments happen and feelings can get hurt. Of course, the recipient can choose not to act on your feedback, but they should never have room to debate the validity of what you're sharing. To do this effectively, focus on your own personal experience of a situation. Describe how someone's actions made you feel, not whether those actions were right or wrong. Only you can know what you felt in a situation, so there really is no room for argument.

Unless you're the boss, giving someone a performance review isn't your job. When you try to share an objective statement about the quality of someone's work, they're more likely to get defensive. Your job, on the other hand, is to help them understand how their actions impacted you. By keeping your commentary focused on your own feelings, your feedback will be more welcomed. To help you navigate the challenges of sharing feedback, I highly recommend using a framework to structure what you want to say in advance.

My favorite is called Situation–Behavior–Impact (SBI), developed by the Center for Creative Leadership. Here's how it works:

1. **Situation:** Describe a specific situation. Avoid broad generalities.
2. **Behavior:** Describe the specific behavior that you're providing feedback on.
3. **Impact:** Describe how the specific behavior *made you feel*.

As you read an example of the SBI model below, imagine that I'm giving you this feedback.

In yesterday's review meeting when you were on your laptop during my presentation, it made me feel that you didn't value my opinion.

- Situation → In yesterday's review meeting...
- Behavior → when you were on your laptop during my presentation,
- Impact → it made me feel that you didn't value my opinion.

Though I'm sure you would never intend to make me feel this way, can you argue the validity of my statement? You can choose to disregard how I felt or refuse to make any changes going forward, but you can't debate my feelings in that moment. By sharing this feedback with you, my goal is for you to hear how your actions made me feel so you can consider what you might want to do differently next time.

Compare that feedback with this:

You're always on your laptop when we're in meetings, and that's why no one thinks you listen to them.

That's how *not* to provide feedback. The same situation can lead to either version of feedback, but the difference is in the delivery. This poorly worded feedback, even if well-intentioned, can lead to a potentially dangerous debate. *I'm not always on my laptop! I do listen to people!* Without the structure that the SBI framework provides, this phrasing is unhelpfully loose, which subtly moves the issue away from understanding and improvement and into debates and defensiveness.

Unfortunately, much of the feedback we give (and receive) is poorly structured and hastily delivered. In many ways, it's our brain seeking shortcuts yet again, the fastest route between idea and execution, regardless of whether it's the best route. When you have feedback to give someone else, take a few minutes and collect your thoughts using the SBI framework. It doesn't take long and will make you much more effective at offering helpful feedback that people actually want to hear.

Give positive feedback

One of the best ways to give more feedback—especially at first while you're getting used to giving it—is to focus on positive feedback. It's the easiest because it's way less scary to tell someone about a great job they did and your praise is pretty unlikely to piss them off. Positive feedback is also productive. It's helpful to share what you feel someone did well so they can focus on doing more of it. Don't just say "Great job!" Use the SBI framework to specifically call out what they did and how it made you feel.

Here's an example: *In yesterday's review meeting, when you closed your laptop, put your phone away, and took notes during my presentation, it made me feel like a valuable member of our team.*

Even something that feels small to you can make someone else's week or month. Think about how you felt the last time you received really positive feedback. You can give that same feeling to one of your colleagues every day of the week—while increasing the likelihood you'll receive feedback of your own soon.

POSITIVE FEEDBACK IS HIGHLY PRODUCTIVE.

Ask before you give feedback

One final tip to help you share more feedback is to ask in advance. Remember, you're almost certainly underestimating someone's desire to hear your feedback. Rather than assume they don't want to hear what you have to say, ask them and find out for sure. More often than not, I find that people want to hear honest feedback if it will help them do their jobs better. For example, "Hey, Bob. I have some feedback about our meeting earlier today that I hope will be helpful for you. Is now a good time for me to share it with you?"

Notice that you're making a direct request, you're giving them enough context to say yes or no, and you're also respecting their time. Just because you're ready with feedback doesn't mean they're ready to hear it at that moment. Throwing feedback at someone when they're deeply focused on an important deliverable or hangrily running to get something to eat between meetings is not a good idea.

PEOPLE WANT YOUR FEEDBACK, BUT **ASK FIRST ANYWAY.**

Now that you're giving more feedback and increasing the overall supply flowing around your team, we need to make sure enough of it makes its way back to you.

How to get more feedback

As you give more feedback, more of it will naturally come back to you thanks to reciprocity bias. But remember, feedback is just as hard for others to share with you as it is for you to share with them. Even if you bought your coworkers a copy of this book (thank you) and they're reading this chapter right now, they may not have feedback for you when you ask for it. And you should ask for it. Just know that the way you ask for feedback can be the difference between hearing complete silence or a constructive comment you can work with.

Ask for feedback in advance

How often have you asked a colleague for feedback and heard things like, "I don't have any for you right now" or "You're doing great"? It's frustrating to know how much feedback can help you, ask for more of it, and get nothing back. When people don't have feedback for you, it's not usually because they don't want to help—it's because they don't have feedback prepared in that moment. Unless you happen to catch them with feedback they were waiting to give you, a broad question like, "Do you have any feedback for me?" is unlikely to result in anything useful.

Instead, ask people for feedback specifically and in advance. For example, before you start a meeting, tell people you're going to ask them for feedback about your presentation at the end. That way, they're primed to pay attention for potential feedback. Asking in advance gives people the chance to prepare and makes it easier for them to share it with you because they know you want to hear it. A little advance notice can make all the difference.

ASK FOR FEEDBACK **SPECIFICALLY,** AND IN **ADVANCE,** TO GET MORE FEEDBACK.

Listen to understand

When someone gives you feedback, they're doing something that isn't easy. They're going out of their way to help you, and if you make it any harder on them, they'll simply stop giving you feedback. Remember, feedback isn't about right and wrong. When receiving feedback, focus on listening and making sure you understand, not debating whether the feedback is justified. Avoid arguing at all costs. You owe it to the other person to hear their feedback. You do not need to agree with it. So long as you listen genuinely, drop your defensiveness and truly consider what they've taken the time and risk to tell you, whether or not you do anything about their feedback is up to you.

Close with gratitude

Try to end every feedback conversation with gratitude. A simple thank you goes a long way. When you take feedback well, especially when it's hard for you to hear, you show people that the risk of sharing feedback with you is low. So they'll share even more later. If you feel that someone gave you bad feedback—meaning poorly delivered, not that it was painful for you to recognize—you can always give them feedback on how you like to get feedback. In fact, getting feedback on your feedback is one of the best ways to improve feedback quality and keep it flowing freely around your team.

How to keep feedback flowing

Let's be honest, free-flowing feedback is not normal. You don't end a Saturday night dinner with your friends by going around the table (as you're all enjoying reciprocity-inducing mints) telling each of them how they made you feel throughout the meal. If you did, you might not have many friends for long. Work is different. Feedback on your performance can help you improve, and the better you do, the better your team and company does. Yes, feedback at work is hard. But unlike at the dinner table, regular feedback has a place on every project.

Once you start giving and receiving more feedback, you'll want to find a way to keep it flowing. You'll also start looking for ways to make feedback even more helpful. For that, we'll go back to Cam and what happened after he was hit with hard feedback about his full day offsite at Shopify. He knew that a classroom setting wasn't going to make feedback stick. People would learn new techniques, try them out for a few days or weeks, but ultimately their focus would fade. He needed feedback to become a habit, part of Shopify's culture.

Fortunately for me, I didn't have to endure the snowstorm training debacle that Cam experienced, nor did I have to get ripped a new one to learn about the tactic they deployed. When I asked Cam how they made feedback a normal part of everyone's day at Shopify, he told me about an exercise that I've used ever since to improve my own feedback and help others to do the same. Like any other skill, the more you practice feedback, the better and more comfortable you get with it. Their exercise works so well because it provides a safe space to improve feedback skills, while making sharing feedback feel like a completely normal thing to do.

The feedback triad is a meeting of three people where each person gives feedback, gets feedback, and observes feedback. Because it's scheduled in advance, everyone comes in expecting to hear feedback and the risk of offending anyone is low. They're easy to run, so you can do them any time. I recommend doing one roughly once every month. You'll leave having not just practiced your feedback skills, but you'll also have received at least two pieces of useful feedback—further increasing the feedback supply.

To get one going, find two colleagues you regularly work with and schedule a meeting in about a week. This will give you all time to prepare feedback for each other, which you should do using the SBI framework.

Here's a sketch of what a triad looks like:

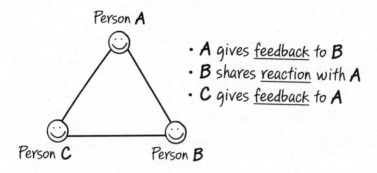

The Feedback Triad

Person A

- **A** gives <u>feedback</u> to **B**
- **B** shares <u>reaction</u> with **A**
- **C** gives <u>feedback</u> to **A**

Person C   Person B

Here's how to run the exercise:

1. Giver gives feedback to the receiver, while the observer watches the interaction.

2. Receiver tells the giver their reaction to the feedback: if they understood it, and how it made them feel.

3. Observer shares feedback with the giver on how they delivered their feedback.

4. Giver listens to the reaction and feedback, asking any clarifying questions they may have, but does not otherwise respond.

5. Move to the next round, rotate participants, and repeat until everyone has played each role.

All you need is a single triad to see why the practice is so powerful. Having someone observe you giving and receiving feedback might feel odd at first, but there's no better way to improve your skills. It's rare to get feedback on your feedback throughout the course of a regular day. Plus, it's not only your feedback giving and receiving that will get better during a triad. Because each person prepared for the meeting, you'll also get real feedback about recent work that you can use to progress and improve yourself.

When the meeting is done, ask each participant to schedule their own triad with two new people. This way, the feedback practice will spread across your whole team. As it does, feedback will feel more and more normal. That supply shortage you used to have will become a surplus.

Full of feedback

The more feedback you get, the faster you'll progress. The challenge is that despite wanting more feedback, few of us actually get enough. Most offices have a feedback supply shortage. There isn't enough to go around. This happens because we overestimate the risks and underestimate the benefits of our feedback, so we tend to keep it to ourselves. Since everyone is just as worried about sharing feedback with you as you are with them, no one gets as much as they need. That's why you have to give more feedback if you want to get more feedback. Aside from increasing the overall supply of feedback on your team, the more you give it, the more others will feel they owe you feedback in return.

To help make it easier for you to give more feedback, reduce the risk and better land what you want to say, use the Situation-Behavior-Impact framework:

- **Situation:** Describe a specific situation. Avoid broad generalities.
- **Behavior:** Describe the specific behavior that you're providing feedback on.
- **Impact:** Describe how the specific behavior *made you feel*.

Think about sharing positive feedback when you're just getting started. It's the easiest, least risky feedback to give—and it usually feels the best, too. As you share more feedback, you'll start to notice more feedback coming back to you. You can get even more by asking people for specific feedback about something you're about to do before you do it. And finally, use a triad to improve your feedback and keep it flowing freely around your team.

When feedback becomes a regular part of your day-to-day, you'll progress faster than you thought possible. Sometimes it will be hard for you to hear. But, just like it did for Cam, even (especially) tough comments can lead to something constructive. On the bright side, if you get hard feedback that makes you feel like you've been ripped a new one, at least you'll have a use for all that extra toilet paper you stockpiled.

ACTION EXERCISE

Schedule and run a feedback triad with two of your colleagues within the next two weeks.

- Explain the exercise and the SBI framework to them in advance (or just buy them a copy of this book—again, thank you).
- When it's done, think about what you learned and how you can share more feedback going forward.

Further reading in case you feel like it

- *Radical Candor: Be a Kick-Ass Boss Without Losing Your Humanity*, Kim Scott—In this book, Scott presents a framework for delivering feedback in a way that balances care for individuals with direct and honest communication. It offers valuable insights on how to provide feedback that is both kind and clear.

- *No Rules Rules*, Reed Hastings and Erin Meyer—Fostering open and honest feedback is a big part of Netflix's culture. Read about how Netflix does feedback and a whole bunch of other key corporate characteristics in this book about the iconic brand.

- *Why We Sleep*, Matthew Walker—Honestly, this book is not about feedback at all. Instead, it's about sleep and how to get better at it. I included it here because, other than being a really great book, few things will help you take difficult feedback better than a good night's sleep.

THE IMPOSSIBLE 10X REQUEST

How to See Opportunities Everyone Else Misses

The only limit to our realization of tomorrow will be our doubts of today.

—FRANKLIN D. ROOSEVELT

The year was 2015 and the internet was ablaze with a global debate about whether #TheDress was white and gold or black and blue. I'm not big into social media, but I remember that moment clearly because there was no debate about the state of my self-confidence at the time: definitely black and blue.

I'd just crashed the startup I cofounded. I felt less than useless. I had let down employees, my family, customers, investors, and my cofounder (the list goes on). My confidence was at an all-time low. By my math, I was done. I had torpedoed my career and no one would ever want to work with, let alone hire, a failure like me ever again.

Fortunately, one of my investors, whose money I'd almost entirely lost, thought enough of me despite the crash to introduce me to "an interesting new team." That team turned out to be Airbnb in its earlier days, and I wound up joining to lead growth in Canada, a market Airbnb was just beginning to enter.

Things were looking up. Maybe I could see some #gold in that dress after all.

Still, my bruised ego motivated me to make an especially strong first impression. I had to show my new team—and, more importantly, myself—that I wasn't my most recent failure. I attacked my first major task, coming up with a plan for Airbnb's growth in Canada that year, with everything I had. I poured in a ton of time, energy, and all of the hard-won lessons I had learned to draft an initial plan I thought was possible, then added a 25 percent stretch target on top to round out what I felt was an aggressive strategy. I packaged it all up into a presentation and hopped on a six-hour flight to Airbnb's headquarters in San Francisco to share how we were going to win the market up north.

I'll never forget that meeting.

I spoke for forty minutes, carefully laying out the detailed plan I'd worked hard on. Everyone was listening intently, but because no one was asking any questions, the room was hard to read. When I was done, I got four seconds of feedback: "This is a fantastic plan. We want you to do ten times the results with ten percent more budget."

Everyone closed their laptops. Meeting over. I stood alone and confused about what had just happened. How good could the plan really have been if they wanted results ten times better? Whether or not that was even possible, how on earth could it be done with only 10 percent more budget? That's definitely impossible.

You know the part in those cartoons featuring Wile E. Coyote and the Roadrunner when Wile E. runs off a cliff but he's suspended in midair until he realizes he's not on solid ground anymore?

The forest before you

The problem is, thanks to confirmation bias and a simple trick of language, we're holding ourselves back every single day without realizing it. Opportunities to advance more quickly, both in terms of professional accomplishment and personal growth, are all around us. We just miss them. We're often blind to our biggest opportunities, which is probably why conventional wisdom is filled with inspirational quotes to help us open our eyes.

Think outside the box. Break the mold. See the forest for the trees.

These sayings sound nice, but they provide no practical help at all. Nothing to tell us what we should actually do differently. I've never intentionally set out to be narrow-minded, fit inside someone else's idea of the status quo, or stare at a tree so long I forget the forest surrounding it. If you want to progress and push the boundaries of what you're capable of, you need something more tangible to help you recognize opportunities you'd otherwise miss.

You'll do this by asking a remarkably simple question, the single most valuable question I have ever learned. Asking it has changed my life. That's not an overstatement. A single question increased my impact at work nearly tenfold, helped me find joy after losing my sister, and motivated me to write this book. I know it can open doors in your life as well.

This simple, tangible tactic will allow you to see the life-changing opportunities you and others are missing. While everyone else is focused on that one tree, you'll see the opportunities throughout the entire forest.

Fir real. (Too much?)

Impossible is more possible than you think

When Airbnb asked me to 10x my plan with just 10 percent more budget, I immediately thought, *That's impossible!* And that was the problem. Consider the last time someone told you something was impossible, or the last time you told yourself, *I can't do that.* Did you think to explore further? Did you ask why, or whether it truly was impossible, rather than simply hard?

The moment you hear the word *can't*, confirmation bias kicks in. This particular unconscious bias, yet another of the 180 we all have, unknowingly leads you to look for or interpret information that is consistent with what you already believe. Rather than exploring potential, when we hear *can't*, our brains actively avoid the possibility and we move on. All it takes for us to succumb to this opportunity blindness is the briefest of thoughts or passing comments. If the first thing you think or hear is that something can't be done, you'll be primed with that belief and seldom, if ever, question it. Worse, you're likely to subconsciously reinforce the belief, making a potentially possible objective feel even less likely. You miss promising opportunities when the first thing you hear is that it can't be done.

Here's the truth: very few achievements are impossible.

But the flip side is this: many achievements aren't feasible.

The key to seeing opportunities others miss is differentiating between possibility and feasibility. People regularly say something *can't* be done when they really mean it *shouldn't* be done. This subtle difference makes all the difference.

CAN'T CLOSES DOORS. **SHOULDN'T KEEPS THEM OPEN FOR DEBATE.**

We use impossibility words like *can't*, *won't*, *never*, and *not possible* all the time. Used correctly, they're about laws, i.e., what's impossible due to the laws of nature or practically not doable because of the laws of society. Want to know whether something is truly impossible? Just ask yourself what law you'd have to break to make it happen. If a law isn't involved, an opportunity may not be right to pursue, but it certainly isn't impossible.

Facing a truly impossible task at work is rare, but nevertheless, we regularly use declarative impossibility language like *can't* or *not possible*. We say something can't be done when really we mean it shouldn't be attempted because it's too hard, unlikely, or expensive. *Can't* is about possibility; *shouldn't* is about feasibility. *Can't* actually cannot be done, no matter how hard we try. *Shouldn't* is possible— we just might choose not to try. Calling out this difference might seem pedantic, but it isn't. Hearing *can't* instead of *shouldn't* is all it takes to activate confirmation bias. Once you're on the lookout for mistakenly using impossibility words instead of feasibility words, you'll see and hear them everywhere, both in your own speech and in others'. I fell into this trap before I realized its impact on my life.

My first thought after hearing the feedback about my plan for Airbnb in Canada was that I *can't* get 10x more results with only 10 percent more budget. That it was impossible. I didn't know it at the time, but I had primed myself to blindly confirm the task couldn't be done. I needed to look at the problem differently and find the opportunities I wasn't seeing. And that came down to our one simple question.

The question you should be asking all the time

To see opportunities others are missing, ask yourself: What would need to be true?

When you're faced with a hard goal—something that can't be done or an idea someone else thinks is never going to happen— make a conscious effort to stop and think. Move from declarative statements about impossibility to exploratory conversations about feasibility. No matter how hard an objective may seem, take a moment to suspend your disbelief and consider "What *would* need to be true?"

This works because that single question shifts your focus from confirming all the reasons an opportunity won't work to exploring the specific details that would need to be true to make it happen. The question forces you to actively consider the possibilities. Once you have a tangible list of what would need to be true (a tactic I'll shortly elaborate on), you can more consciously decide what to do next. The best hidden opportunities tend to have endless reasons why they won't work. That's why you need to stop and force yourself to think about what would need to be true. Without doing so, you're missing around half the information you need to evaluate whether or not it's worth trying.

Declarative statements about impossibility like *can't* and *not possible* are warning signs that you're about to miss an opportunity—maybe even a life-changing moment. When you think them or hear them, that's when it's time to stop and ask, "What would need to be true?"

LISTEN FOR WORDS LIKE **CAN'T** AND **WON'T**, THEN ASK, **"WHAT WOULD NEED TO BE TRUE?"**

The point isn't to run after every single crazy idea. Some achievements truly are impossible. Even if they aren't, it may not make sense to try. An objective might take too much money or too much time or be too risky. In these cases, you're right to move on. You don't need to attempt everything just because someone else said it's impossible. Rather, your goal is to make a conscious effort to bring feasibility to the forefront of your mind for any "impossible" problem in need of a creative solution. You may, in fact, decide not to pursue the initiative, but at least you're doing so on purpose, based on an assessment of the details and not on someone else's opinion or your own self-limiting biases. More often than not, however, I find that what previously felt impossible and would otherwise have been ignored gets serious consideration after asking, *"What would need to be true?"*

Missing these opportunities is so common and happens so outside of your day-to-day awareness that it's important to have a simple tactic to follow—something you can cultivate into a habit to the point where your new normal becomes uncovering overlooked opportunities rather than blowing right by them.

How to use "What would need to be true?"

For any challenge, and particularly those that feel hard or impossible, follow these steps:

1. Listen for declarative impossibility words like *can't*, *won't*, *never*, and *not possible*.
2. When you hear or think any of those words, immediately stop and ask, "What would need to be true?" and write out a list. Don't bother with what won't work (that's for later). Simply focus on what would actually need to be true if you assumed your objective was, in fact, possible.
3. Based on that list, decide whether or not to move forward. Use the factors routine from Chapter 7 to help you make your decision.

Again, your ultimate decision isn't the point. What matters is that you choose *purposefully*. Remember: you're working to avoid confirmation bias and the common situation where you think or hear something can't be done and never truly consider trying.

Exploring new opportunities is even more valuable when others, like your boss or teammates, get involved. Having an initial list of what would need to be true will help you bring them into the exercise. When you get pushback—and you will get pushback because it "can't" be done—politely ask people to park the conversation about possibility for a moment. Say,

> *"I understand that we've talked about all the reasons it won't work. Can you humor me for a moment and let me know what you think <u>would</u> need to be true?"*

Try to get to the point of having an actual list you can all look at together, then revisit the discussion with that specific list in mind to decide whether or not to try.

If you do decide to pursue the project, plan, or opportunity further, odds are good that it's not going to be easy. You might get stuck looking at your list thinking, *How am I supposed to get any of these things done?* If that happens, keep asking yourself "What would need to be true?" to figure out next steps you can take action on:

1. Write out a list of what would need to be true.
2. If any items in that list feel doable, pick one and do it.
3. If you "can't" do any of them, ask "What would need to be true?" for each item on your list.

4. Repeat steps 2 and 3, working your way down into increasingly more granular answers, until you hit something you think you can get done.

5. Go do the first task that feels feasible (worry about what to do after that once it's done).

The idea is to break down a big, challenging objective into the component parts that need to be true so you can accomplish them one small step at a time. Don't worry if you can't see the entire plan right away. Just get started. You'll feel differently and learn more about what to do next once you've taken a first step. The sooner you get moving, the sooner you'll learn whether your objective truly can be accomplished. So let's see how I applied the theory of "What would need to be true?" to my 10x impossible request.

A case study in what would need to be true

After snapping out of my initial Wile E. Coyote moment, I spent the rest of my trip flipping back and forth between the excitement of meeting all the incredible new people I'd have the privilege of working with, and the deep-seated dread that I had already failed and wouldn't be around them much longer. The plan and meeting I hoped would bring a much-needed confidence boost pulled me down further. I was shell-shocked, doubting myself on all fronts.

But on the plane ride home, I reminded myself that I joined Airbnb on purpose. *I might as well try something new and see what happens.* I also figured that if I was going to go down, I might as well go down big. And then I asked myself a different question—one you should know by now.

Up until that moment, I had been fixated on all of the very logical reasons why what I was being asked to do couldn't be done. Writing on a small notepad atop a tiny foldaway airplane tray, I forced myself to try a different approach. To consider the possibilities. I asked myself, "What would need to be true for us to achieve 10x more growth with 10 percent more budget?" The list started with the essentials.

To achieve 10x more growth with 10 percent more budget, it would need to be true that we:

- Reach 10x more people
- Convince them to try Airbnb

But how? So I asked the question again about each answer.

- What would need to be true to reach a lot more people?
- What would need to be true to convince them to try Airbnb?

This resulted in a longer list.

- To **reach ten times more people,** it would need to be true that we:
  - Run more advertisements
  - Partner with third parties (companies, influencers, etc.) that have aligned audiences
  - Run events for potential customers
  - Increase unpaid media attention (e.g., mentions in the news)

- **To convince them to try Airbnb**, it would need to be true that:
  - People we reach are interested in traveling
  - We articulate Airbnb's value well
  - We provide an incentive to get them to try Airbnb for the first time

My opinion completely changed after finishing this list. I'd only asked this unlocking question three times and already felt relief. What had seemed wholly impossible just a few days ago seemed at least approachable now. I could confidently explore the feasibility of the problem.

Right off the bat, I saw that the key challenge was going to be reaching 10x more people. Though I knew we'd also have to convince them to try Airbnb, we had evidence from work in other countries to suggest that would be doable, so long as we increased our reach. Though certainly a hard problem, I had already thought a lot about how to increase our reach, and the push to use only 10 percent more budget actually became a helpful constraint.

Knowing that we couldn't spend much more money allowed me to quickly cull options.

- **To reach ten times more people**, it would need to be true that we:
  - Run more advertisements → too expensive
  - Partner with third parties (companies, influencers, etc.) that have aligned audiences → feasible
  - Run events for potential customers → too expensive
  - Increase unpaid media attention → feasible

When the plane landed, I rushed home to get my thinking down into a presentation I shared with my team the next day. We decided to focus on third-party partnerships and unpaid media attention, given their potential for increasing reach without much additional budget. And that's how Bruce Springsteen almost ruined my life. I mean, that's how we eventually hosted our *Night At* event, reaching millions who saw the (unpaid) news coverage of the first-of-its-kind sleepover. Our new possibility-driven perspective led to the idea for the *Night At* and many other initiatives we never would have thought to try if we had stopped at "can't."

Fast-forward to the end of the year. We didn't quite 10x the initial plan, but we got pretty close. Remember that 25 percent stretch target I had added on top of what I thought was possible just to make sure the plan looked aggressive enough? We beat it many times over. Instead of working forward from what felt possible, we worked back from an "impossible" goal, asking what would need to be true at each step along the way.

Unintentionally underperforming

What we accomplished was great, but the real value was what the experience taught me. The only appreciable difference between the first and second plan was mindset. I certainly wasn't any smarter after asking that simple question multiple times. Our team didn't change either. Rather, we just worked from a different plan built with a different mentality.

This led me to a very uncomfortable but equally important existential question. If all it really took was asking the right question, because I had never asked it before, had I been underachieving by an order of magnitude up until that point in my life?

The inescapable answer was yes.

From then on I became maniacally focused on listening for impossibility words and asking "What would need to be true?" across my entire life. *You can't write a book.* Should I? *You'll never be happy.* What would need to be true? If all you take away from this book is how to ask "What would need to be true?" you'll be in good shape. All of the other tactics I've covered can be derived from it, such as: What would need to be true to make better decisions? What would need to be true to enjoy your job more?

I'm not sure whether Airbnb's leaders intended to impact my entire frame of mind with their four seconds of feedback, but they certainly knew how to get the most out of me. I'm grateful to them to this day.

If you want to see opportunities others miss, listen for *can't*. When you hear it, ask "What would need to be true?"

You may just 10x your impact at work, and in life.

ACTION EXERCISE

For at least the next week, actively listen for declarative impossibility words like *can't*, *won't*, and *not possible* during every meeting you're in. When you hear one, politely stop the conversation and ask the group (or yourself), "What would need to be true?" At the end of the week, reflect on the impact:

- Did you hear any declarative impossibility words?
- Were they truly impossible, or was it actually a question of feasibility?
- Did "What would need to be true?" uncover any potential opportunities you might otherwise have missed?

Further reading in case you feel like it

- *The Innovator's Dilemma: When New Technologies Cause Great Firms to Fail*, C. M. Christensen—This is a classic about how and why businesses fail to see new opportunities so big they wind up turning into entirely new markets.

- *Creativity Inc.*, Edwin Catmull and Amy Wallace—This tells the founding and coming-of-age story of Pixar, with a clear focus on how to build cultures of creativity. There are lots of interesting tactics to help you and your team think differently throughout this book.

- *Where Good Ideas Come From*, Steven Johnson—This book won't tell you how to be more creative, but it will give you an interesting walk through the creation of some of history's biggest innovations.

How to Progress Faster
(Without Waiting for a Promotion)

Chapter 7 **How to make better decisions**

Without you being aware of it, your brain takes shortcuts that hurt your decision-making. The most common approach to decision-making, using a pros and cons list, is not the best way to decide. Use the factors routine to make better decisions:

1. List every relevant factor in your decision.
2. Make a mini-decision based on each factor alone.
3. Make a final decision considering all of the factors together.

Chapter 8 **How to get more feedback**

Feedback is the fuel for your growth and development. Unfortunately, most people don't get enough feedback. The counterintuitive way to get more feedback is to give more of it. Use the SBI framework to make it easier for you to give feedback, so you get more of it in return:

1. Situation: Describe a specific situation. Avoid broad generalities.
2. Behavior: Describe the specific behavior you want to provide feedback on.
3. Impact: Describe how the specific behavior made you feel.

Chapter 9 **How to see opportunities everyone else misses**

Can't and *shouldn't* mean two very different things, but we often use them interchangeably. When you do, you activate confirmation bias in your brain and miss perfectly possible opportunities. What would need to be true?

1. Listen for declarative impossibility words like *can't, won't, never,* and *not possible.*

2. When you hear or think any of those words, immediately stop and ask, "What would need to be true?" and write out a list.

3. Based on that list, decide whether or not to move forward.

CONCLUSION

Gutted, Grateful, and Greener Grass

Now this is not the end. It is not even the beginning of the end. But it is, perhaps, the end of the beginning.

—WINSTON CHURCHILL

Lately, I've found myself noticing little character traits here and there that remind me of my sister. I waved goodbye to a friend and watched my hand move just like hers used to. I didn't even realize she had a particular way of waving before that. The other day, I must have said something interesting to my dad because he stopped to think and made the same noise my sister used to make when she was thinking. I don't remember Rachel having a thinking noise when she was alive, but there it was, right there, coming from my dad. It's been almost five years since she passed away and it's only just now, standing at the end and looking back on her life, that these behavioral bits and pieces reveal themselves to me.

There's something about endings that clarify our journeys in ways we can't see when we're on them.

What are you afraid of?

In a similar way, I've only just started to recognize lessons about myself while standing at the end of my journey writing this book.

One of the biggest changes I notice is with my relationship with speed. I used to think my ability to maintain a fast pace was one of my greatest strengths. It was tied to my ego in a big way. Speed was my edge. Looking back, I realize that I was scared to consider slowing down, advice I had received many times, because I didn't know how I would accomplish all of my ambitions if I stopped pushing so hard. Frankly, I think I was just afraid of losing my edge—a big part of what made me, me.

The fear of losing some critical essence is what I hear most from people when they start thinking about enjoying their jobs more or doing their work differently. Perhaps your edge is how hard you work, your ambition, or a strong track record of upward trajectory. Whatever it is, I can assure you that taking a leap and trying the tactics you've just read will not result in you losing your edge. On the contrary, your new approach to work will be the very thing that sharpens what you're already great at.

So what's preventing you from leaping?

Gutted and grateful

In the months leading up to and following Rachel's death, I took a forced leap of faith. I had to slow down. I didn't know what would happen to my impact or ambition, but it didn't matter. I couldn't cope. What was going on in my life at the time didn't give me a choice. Previously, I assumed that all I could learn from slowing down was how to be OK with accomplishing less. To learn to be OK having less impact in exchange for less effort. I had many assumptions just like that about how I was supposed to work. Because I never really questioned them, I never found a better way.

These days, I work fewer hours, but I get more done than I ever have. I work hard, but I work differently, and I'm loving it. What's interesting is that I didn't need a radical shift to get here. I already had the tools I needed—I just needed to use them differently. As I began finding better and better ways to work, my life overall started to improve. It felt crazy to me that losing my sister could possibly be a positive catalyst. How could I explain that losing my sister was leading to so much positivity in my life?

What I didn't understand at the time was that two competing concepts can both be true at the same time. I can feel both gutted at losing my sister *and* grateful for what I've gained. My experience with grief may feel disconnected from your experience at work, but it's not entirely. Your work can be hard *and* you can enjoy it more at the same time. The job you have right now can be difficult, *and* it can still be your dream job—even if it's not quite there yet.

The secret to better work

Trying to reconcile opposites, rather than recognizing that they can coexist, often leads us to assume our environment needs to change. When you think about work being better, how often do you think of a new project, new team, or new job entirely solving your problems? How many times have you been told that you need to develop some fundamental new skill or create a radical change in your capabilities if you want to progress in your career?

Changing what you do on its own doesn't address the true root challenge if you want to accomplish more and feel better about it along the way. The secret to better work—and a more enjoyable life as a result—is to change *how* you're working. Using the skills you already have to improve the work you already do. This leads to the most lasting change because any improvement in your underlying approach carries forward to the next project, team, or entirely new job you do in the future.

YOU DON'T NEED DIFFERENT WORK TO *FEEL BETTER*, YOU JUST NEED TO **DO THE WORK YOU ALREADY HAVE DIFFERENTLY.**

I'm not suggesting you never change what you do. Your tasks, team, and title are certainly important aspects of your work, and, of course, there are times when changing what you do is necessary— like if you're in a toxic environment or don't feel safe at your office. What I am suggesting is this: don't start by assuming you need a situational change.

The next time you think something new will solve all your problems, try reflecting on how you can better use what you already have instead. Avoid looking at the grass elsewhere and expecting it to magically be greener. You already have a job that can be your dream job; you just need to do it differently. You already have the skills you need to work smarter, not harder. You just need to use them differently. You can already think outside of the box, get a boost from self-doubt, take back control of your own time, and make decisions like the best thinkers in business. Changing how you work will lead you to do your job better and enjoy yourself more along the way. All you needed were a few tactics to help you unlock the potential of what you already have.

You already have what you need

Each of the tactics we covered in the book is different, but they are tied together by a central theme: you. You may have noticed that none of the tactics need anyone else, just you. There's loads of advice out there about focusing on yourself first, but I never really knew what that meant until I reflected on the tactics that were truly helping me. What I hope to have shared with you over the course of this book is a specific and actionable set of techniques you can actually use because they focus entirely on what is in your control to change: your own actions.

To conclude, I'll share the playbook in its entirety.

Consider this the end of the beginning, and the rest is up to you. If you haven't yet already, pick a single tactic and see what happens when you try it out. Keep on the lookout for each of the key challenges we covered, and when they pop up—and pop up they will—jump into the tactic. Rip out these last few pages and stick them to your monitor if it helps. Do whatever you need to do to remind yourself that you—not just your manager, HR representative, or teammates—have the power to change how you're working. Other

YOUR GRASS IS GREENER

people can help you, but you certainly don't need to wait for anyone other than yourself to decide to work differently and transform your job into one of the most positive drivers in your life overall.

You already have everything you need to get what you want at work and in life.

Your grass *is* greener.

216

THE GREENER GRASS

PLAYBOOK

Note: you can download the playbook in its entirety at
www.yourgrassisgreener.com/resources

HOW TO ELIMINATE MISCOMMUNICATION

Challenge	Miscommunications cost you up to a day every week in wasted work. Most miscommunications are invisible—you only learn about them after you've gone in the wrong direction—because you've understood, but misinterpreted.
Key Insight	Effective communication ends when you hear your intent repeated back to you, not when you finish speaking.
Get What You Want	<ul><li>Eliminate miscommunication</li><li>Save up to a day every week</li><li>Stop frustrating repeat work</li></ul>
Using What You Have	<ul><li>Asking a question</li><li>Listening</li><li>Repeating what you hear</li></ul>

Tactic

Use a brief back anytime the potential cost of a miscommunication is too high for you.

Asking for a brief back: *"Can you let me know what you took away from this conversation so I can be sure I did a good job getting my point across?"*

Giving a brief back: *"I think what you just told me is [insert the message you heard]. Did I get that right?"*

Tip

Whether asking for or giving a brief back, keep the focus on you, not them.

HOW TO SPEED UP SLOW DECISION-MAKING

Challenge	We're wired to agree with one another while simultaneously building teams that disagree. Trying to get everyone to agree with every decision is wasting up to a full day of unnecessary work every week.
Key Insight	The better you disagree, the faster you'll decide.
Get What You Want	• Speed up team decisions • Save up to a day every week • Eliminate endless meetings that don't close on decisions
Using What You Have	• Asking a question • Sharing what you know • Supporting a decision

Tactic

1. Ask "Who is deciding?" before debating any decision.
2. Share context, not opinions, in order to avoid groupthink.
3. Seek alignment, not agreement, to move forward even when you can't agree.

Tip

Use a written framework so everyone can see how their context was considered to help them commit to a decision, even when they disagree.

HOW TO TAKE BACK CONTROL OF YOUR TIME

Challenge	It's hard to say no, so you take on too much and work too many hours trying to get it all done. On average, distractions cost you about a day every single week, and not getting everything done drains your energy.
Key Insight	Defining what not to do is how you get more done.
Get What You Want	• Own your own time • Reclaim a full workday of misplaced productivity every week • Get your own work done and feel good about it
Using What You Have	• Writing • An existing to-do list • Asking questions

Tactic

At the start of every week, write a not-to-do list to complement your to-do list:

1. Put your top three most important priorities on your to-do list.
2. Put everything else on your not-to-do list.
3. Only add more to your to-do list if your schedule is wide open after blocking out time for your top three priorities.

Use your lists to help you say no when you need to:

- "I'm prioritizing XYZ, which feels most impactful for me to do right now. Do you see it differently?"
- "I'm prioritizing XYZ right now. What would happen if I got back to you on this by Monday instead?"
- "I'm prioritizing XYZ right now. Is there someone else that could help?"

Tip

Force yourself to take something off your to-do list every time you add something new. Forcing trade-offs will help you be more clear about what you truly need to get done.

HOW TO PROMOTE THE IMPOSTER IN YOU

Challenge	Self-doubt and imposter syndrome can hold you back from doing your best work. Trying to simply turn off your feelings usually leads to feeling and performing even worse.
Key Insight	Imposter syndrome can be a superpower for you.
Get What You Want	<ul><li>A greater sense of belonging on your team</li><li>Increase your self-confidence</li><li>Feel less stress and more freedom day-to-day</li></ul>
Using What You Have	<ul><li>Imposter syndrome</li><li>Asking questions</li><li>One of your existing strengths</li></ul>

Tactic

When you feel imposter syndrome:

1. Ask follow-up questions in one-on-one meetings to learn what you don't know and build stronger relationships in the process.
2. Redirect your focus from what your team does better than you to what you can uniquely bring to them.
3. Once you feel comfortable, start asking more questions in group settings so you can help get the most out of your team.

Tip

Ask questions with a genuine interest to learn, or don't ask them at all.

HOW TO MEASURE YOUR JOY ON THE JOB

Challenge	The more you enjoy your job, the better you do it. Unfortunately, most workplaces focus exclusively on measuring your performance and accomplishments, which are not accurate reflections of how you feel day-to-day.
Key Insight	Joy on the job is measured in your moments, not your milestones.
Get What You Want	• Enjoy your day-to-day job more • Gain a better understanding of what you enjoy doing • See a clearer picture of how much time you spend doing things you enjoy at work
Using What You Have	• Writing • Your calendar

Tactic

Measure your moments at the end of any week:

1. Fold a piece of paper in half lengthwise to create two columns.
2. On one side, write a list of tasks you enjoy doing.
3. On the other side, write a list of everything you actually did this week—referencing your calendar as needed.
4. Unfold the paper and draw a line from tasks you enjoy to any tasks you actually did this week.
5. Then answer: "Do you enjoy your job?"

Tip

Pick one thing from your list of what you enjoy doing and do it tomorrow.

HOW TO UNLOCK MORE JOY AT YOUR JOB

Challenge	You don't get a dream job, you practice it. The challenge is that best practices for one person are rarely best practices for you. Pressures and priorities make it hard for you to work in your own best way.
Key Insight	You don't need to change what you do to enjoy it more.
Get What You Want	<ul><li>Enjoy your job more</li><li>Perform better at work</li><li>Feel better across the rest of your life</li></ul>
Using What You Have	<ul><li>Writing</li><li>Self-reflection</li></ul>

Tactic

Before you start a task, use your career compass to guide your best approach to any task: doing something you love, leveraging an existing skill, learning a new one, and doing less of what you don't enjoy doing.

To create your compass, answer these questions:
- What do you love doing?
- What are you great at?
- Where do you want to improve?
- What do you not love doing?
- What are you not great at?
- Where do you not want to improve?

Then map your answers to the four points of your career compass using the template at www.yourgrassisgreener.com/resources.

Tip

Schedule regular reviews with your manager to keep your career compass up to date. This helps you trust your compass more, question it less, and keep focused on your moments.

HOW TO MAKE BETTER DECISIONS

Challenge	Without you being aware of it, your brain takes shortcuts that hurt your decision-making. The most common approach to decision-making, using a pros and cons list, is not the best way to decide.
Key Insight	Using a routine for your thinking helps you avoid unconscious biases.
Get What You Want	• Have more intentional, less biased thinking • Make better decisions at work and in life • Achieve better outcomes more often
Using What You Have	• Rational analysis • Your feelings • Writing

Tactic

Use the factors routine to make better decisions:

1. List every relevant factor in your decision.
2. Make a mini-decision based on each factor alone.
3. Make a final decision considering all of the factors together.

Tip

Include your gut feel as a factor. Be sure to cool off any big emotions before making a final decision. Use the framework at www.yourgrassisgreener.com/resources to help you make the best decisions possible.

HOW TO GET MORE FEEDBACK

Challenge	Feedback is the fuel for your growth and development. Unfortunately, very few people get enough feedback because giving feedback is hard. You give less feedback to others than you could, and they give less than they could to you.
Key Insight	The more feedback you give, the more feedback you'll get.
Get What You Want	<ul><li>Get more feedback</li><li>Get better feedback</li><li>Experience more (and faster) personal and professional progression</li></ul>
Using What You Have	<ul><li>Rational analysis</li><li>Your feelings</li><li>Writing</li></ul>

Tactic

Use the SBI framework to make it easier for you to give feedback, so you get more of it in return:

1. Situation: Describe a specific situation. Avoid broad generalities.
2. Behavior: Describe the specific behavior you want to provide feedback on.
3. Impact: Describe how the specific behavior made you feel.

Tip

Giving feedback

- Use the SBI model to structure your feedback
- Share positive feedback
- Always ask before sharing any feedback

Getting feedback

- Ask for feedback in advance
- Listen to understand
- Close with gratitude

HOW TO SEE OPPORTUNITIES EVERYONE ELSE MISSES

Challenge	*Can't* and *shouldn't* mean two very different things, but we often use them interchangeably. When we do, we activate confirmation bias in our brains and miss perfectly possible opportunities without even noticing, let alone thinking to try.
Key Insight	Asking "What would need to be true?" reduces confirmation bias and opens your mind to the potential of accomplishing more than you previously thought possible.
Get What You Want	• See more opportunities • Find more creative solutions • Have more impact
Using What You Have	• Asking a question

Tactic

1. Listen for declarative impossibility words like *can't, won't, never*, and *not possible*.
2. When you hear or think any of those words, immediately stop and ask, "What would need to be true?" and write out a list.
3. Based on that list, decide whether or not to move forward.

Tip

If you decide to pursue the opportunity further, use "What would need to be true?" to break the challenge down and figure out your next steps:

1. Write out a list of what would need to be true.
2. If any items in that list feel doable, pick one and do it.
3. If you "can't" do any of them, ask, "What would need to be true?" for each item on your list.
4. Repeat steps 2 and 3 until you hit something you think you can get done.
5. Go do that thing (worry about what to do after that once it's done).

GRATITUDE

Taking a page from my own book, I thought rhyming my thank-yous would be more enjoyable to write (and hopeful to read as well).

Rachel, I miss you and I'm grateful for everything we ever did together.
The impact of your life on mine is truly impossible to measure.
You're still having an incredible impact on me, my life, and our family, and you always will. I know you'll never read these words, but that doesn't make them any less true.

To my wife, Idana, there is no way this book would exist without you.
You helped me even when talking about writing was the last thing you wanted to do.
From helping me weed out the bad ideas from the good ones to sharing your input on a hundred different title options, you were a huge help. Thanks for supporting this book more than I did at times.

Blake Atwood, you're easily one of the greatest editors on this planet,
I'm grateful you chose to work with me after your success with *Atomic Habit*(s).
Thank you for representing the voice of the reader and entertaining my lengthy debates about problem statements. Your fingerprints are all over this book, and I've become a better writer and communicator thanks to you.

To Megan, Andrew, Katharine, Sarah, Jordan, and Cam.
You're all the best for letting me share your stories, I can't tell you how grateful I am.
From the start I knew I wanted to tell real people's stories. That you were game to share yours with an unknown audience simply because it might help them says a lot about all of you.

Steve, when my sister was sick you were the kindest boss I could have asked for.
You went above and beyond to support me, you really couldn't have done more.
I know it wasn't easy for you to support me in the way you did back in the early days of integrate.ai. I'm sure it created stress and more work for you, but you never showed it. I'm grateful for our relationship both then and now.

The entire Ideapress team helped turn my manuscript into a book you can buy.
Look further for a better publisher? There's no reason to try.
Thank you Rohit, Marnie, Megan, Allison, and Kameron for all of your hard work and dedication to make my book a reality. You added a ton of value across the board and were really fun to work with too!

So many people read early drafts and gave me feedback about it.
Thanks for using kind words when you thought my writing was shi...not good.
Special shout-outs to John Duff, Courtney Cooper, Adam Jarczyn, Matt Urback, Jay Rosenzweig, and Bob Brehl for giving me the boost I needed in the early days.

Cam Gregg, I could say thanks to you across nearly every aspect of my life.
You have a special talent for words that cut through confusion like a knife.
Thank you for helping me keep my head on straight over the past many years. You've been an invaluable resource for me both at work and in life. You're a true friend.

I'd need a whole other book to list everyone that helped with the title.
We went through so many options, and your feedback was vital.
Thanks in particular to Megan Seres, Anant Gadia, Brett Preston, Sandra Preston, Meagan Cooper, James Cutler, Sandra Veledar, and Adam Neal.

I remember the first time I thought, wow, this looks like a real book.
It happened when I got draft designs so I could have a quick look.
To Jessica Angerstein and David Fassett, thanks for finding the right visual representation of the book. From cover iterations to interior illustrations, you were both awesome.

Mom and Dad. What a cliche to thank my parents at the end of my book.
Thanks for parenting me so well that I didn't turn out to be a crook.
Mom, your notes on my writing were really helpful, and Dad, having you to bounce marketing ideas off of was amazing. I'm grateful to have both of you in my life. There's a hole in our family, but Rachel would be proud to see how we've grown.

And finally to you, the reader.
Thanks for trying the tactics and remember: your grass is greener.

CONNECT WITH JASON

I enjoy meeting new people and would love to hear from you. The best way to get in touch with me in general is via my website at www.thejasonsilver.com/contact. Below are a few more specific reasons many people reach out to me.

You want to buy copies of my book for your team or company

All of the tactics you just read get even better when everyone at work is practicing them with you. If you're interested in buying multiple copies of the book for a reading group, your team, or entire company, I'd be happy to discuss bulk discounts and special offers for you.

Contact: **hello@thejasonsilver.com**

You're interested in having me speak or run a workshop

From speeding up slow team decision-making to eliminating miscommunications across entire organizations, I can deliver a workshop or talk to your team or company on the tactics from the book. I also love giving keynotes at the right conferences too. Your audience will leave entertained, and with a tangible tactic they can immediately try at work.

To learn more, check out: **www.thejasonsilver.com**
Or inquire directly at: **hello@thejasonsilver.com**

You want more tactics

Every few weeks I publish a newsletter with new tactics to help you do and feel better at work. Each article always includes a true story, a tangible tactic, and a terrible joke you can try not to laugh at. Sign-up is free and comes with exclusive bonuses.

Join colleagues across countless companies here:
thejasonsilver.com/newsletter

You have feedback you'd like to share with me

I'd love to hear from you with any feedback you have about the book. Did you love it? Not so much? Have ideas for other helpful tactics you'd like to discuss?

Drop me a line: **hello@thejasonsilver.com**

You just want to say hi!

thejasonsilver.com
hello@thejasonsilver.com
in linkedin.com/in/silverjay

ADDITIONAL RESOURCES

All of the guides, templates, prompts, and playbooks mentioned throughout *Your Grass Is Greener* can be downloaded for free here: **www.yourgrassisgreener.com/resources**

You'll also find plenty of bonus content not mentioned in the book.

NOTES

INTRODUCTION

Page 6 **a nice perk:** Judge, Timothy A., Joyce E. Bono, Amir Erez, and Edwin A. Locke. "Core Self-Evaluations and Job and Life Satisfaction: The Role of Self-Concordance and Goal Attainment." *Journal of Applied Psychology* 90, no. 2 (March 2005): 257–68. https://pubmed.ncbi.nlm.nih.gov/15769236/.

Amabile, T. M., S. G. Barsade, J. S. Mueller, and B. M. Staw. "Affect and Creativity at Work." *Administrative Science Quarterly* 50, no. 3 (2005): 367–403. https://journals.sagepub.com/doi/10.2189/asqu.2005.50.3.367.

Shimazu, Akihito, Wilmar B. Schaufeli, Kimika Kamiyama, and Norito Kawakami. "Workaholism vs. Work Engagement: The Two Different Predictors of Future Well-Being and Performance." *International Journal of Behavioral Medicine* 22, no. 1 (February 2015): 18–23. https://pubmed.ncbi.nlm.nih.gov/24696043/.

Faragher, E. B., M. Cass, and C. L. Cooper. "The Relationship between Job Satisfaction and Health: A Meta-Analysis." *Occupational and Environmental Medicine* 62, no. 2 (February 2005): 105–12. https://pubmed.ncbi.nlm.nih.gov/15657192/.

O'Keefe, Paul A. "Liking Work Really Matters." *New York Times*, September 5, 2014. https://www.nytimes.com/2014/09/07/opinion/sunday/go-with-the-flow.html?_r=0.

O'Keefe, Paul A. "The Role of Interest in Optimizing Performance and Self-Regulation." *Journal of Experimental Social Psychology* 53, no. 53 (July 2014): 70-78. https://www.sciencedirect.com/science/article/abs/pii/S002210311400016X.

Pollack, Jeffrey M., Violet T. Ho, Ernest H. O'Boyle, and Bradley L. Kirkman. "Passion at Work: A Meta-Analysis of Individual Work Outcomes." *Journal of Organizational Behavior* 41, no. 4 (May 2020): 311-331. https://onlinelibrary.wiley.com/doi/10.1002/job.2434.

Kwon, Mijeong, Julia Lee Cunningham, and Jon M. Jachimowicz. "Discerning Saints: Moralization of Intrinsic Motivation and Selective Prosociality at Work." *Academy of Management Journal* 66, no. 6 (December 2023). https://journals.aom.org/doi/abs/10.5465/amj.2020.1761.

Page 7 **eight in ten feel regret:** Human Resources. "Employee Regret after the Great Resignation." *Paychex,* January 16, 2023. https://www.paychex.com/articles/human-resources/exploring-the-great-regret.

Page 8 **struggling in their lives overall:** Gallup. "Employee Wellbeing." *Gallup,* 2024. https://www.gallup.com/394424/indicator-employee-well-being.aspx.

Harter, Jim. "Globally, Employees Are More Engaged—and More Stressed." *Gallup,* June 2023. https://www.gallup.com/workplace/506798/globally-employees-engaged-stressed.aspx.

Page 11 **Productivity is lower than ever:** Storeconnect. "Worker Productivity in the U.S. Is at an All-Time Low: Who or What Is to Blame?" *PRWeb,* June 5, 2023. https://www.prweb.com/releases/worker-productivity-in-the-u-s-is-at-an-all-time-low-who-or-what-is-to-blame--895743764.html.

Page 11 **once at their current job:** Fisher, Jen. "Workplace Burnout Survey." *Deloitte,* 2015. https://www2.deloitte.com/us/en/pages/about-deloitte/articles/burnout-survey.html.

Page 11 **disengaged from work:** Gallup. "State of the Global Workplace: 2023 Report." *Gallup,* 2023. https://www.gallup.com/workplace/349484/state-of-the-global-workplace.aspx.

Page 12 **their well-being overall:** Fisher, Jen, Colleen Bordeaux, Paul H. Silverglate, and Michael Gilmartin. "As Workforce Well-Being Dips, Leaders Ask: What Will It Take to Move the Needle?" *Deloitte,* June 20, 2023. https://www2.deloitte.com/xe/en/insights/topics/talent/workplace-well-being-research.html.

PART 1: UNBLOCK

CHAPTER 1: The Day Springsteen Nearly Crashed My Career: How to Eliminate Miscommunication

Page 21 **and flannel sheets:** Airbnb. "Airbnb Teams Up with Toronto Maple Leafs and Toronto Raptors to Offer Overnight Experience at Air Canada Centre." *Cision.* November 2015. https://www.newswire.ca/news-releases/airbnb-teams-up-with-toronto-maple-leafs-and-toronto-raptors-to-offer-overnight-experience-at-air-canada-centre-550967911.html.

Page 22 **a pregame shootaround:** Airbnb. "Night at Air Canada Centre." YouTube Video. February 2016. https://www.youtube.com/watch?v=DOLJHF59z7s.

Page 23 **trillion every year:** Grammarly. "The State of Business Communication." *Grammarly*, 2022. https://www.grammarly.com/business/Grammarly_The_State_Of_Business_Communication.pdf.

Page 23 **that staggering number:** The World Bank. "GDP (Current US$)." *The World Bank*, 2024. https://data.worldbank.org/indicator/NY.GDP.MKTP.CD?most_recent_value_desc=true.

Page 23 **stressed or anxious:** Grammarly. "Poor Communication Causes Work Stress—Here's Why You Need to Address It Now." *Grammarly* (Blog). *Grammarly.* February 21, 2023. https://www.grammarly.com/blog/poor-communication-work-stress/.

Page 23 **miscommunication in the workplace:** Grammarly. "Poor Communication Causes Work Stress—Here's Why You Need to Address It Now." *Grammarly* (Blog). *Grammarly.* February 21, 2023. https://www.grammarly.com/blog/poor-communication-work-stress/.

CHAPTER 2: Too Many Cooks in the Kitchen: How to Speed Up Slow Decision-Making

Page 41 **of 400,000 people:** NASA. "The First Step: Langley's Contributions to Apollo." *NASA*, March 22, 2019. https://www.nasa.gov/history/the-first-step-langleys-contributions-to-apollo/.

Hollingham, Richard. "Apollo in 50 Numbers: The workers." *BBC*, June 19, 2019. https://www.bbc.com/future/article/20190617-apollo-in-50-numbers-the-workers.

Page 41 **over $250 billion:** Dreier, Casey. "An Improved Cost Analysis of the Apollo Program." *Space Policy* 60, (May 2022). https://www.sciencedirect.com/science/article/pii/S0265964622000029.

Page 41 **One single day:** McChrystal, Stanley, Tantum Collins, David Silverman, and Chris Fussell. *Team of Teams: New Rules of Engagement for a Complex World*. New York: Portfolio/Penguin, 2015.

Page 42 **humans 768,800 kilometers:** Mortillaro, Nicole. "Looking Back to Apollo 11: How We Did So Much with So Little." *CBC News*, July 20, 2019. https://www.cbc.ca/news/science/apollo-11-tech-1.5208758.

Page 42 **3 million parts:** Popular Mechanics. "Saturn V Is the Biggest Engine Ever Built." *Popular Mechanics*, December 6, 2004. https://www.popularmechanics.com/science/a227/1280801/.

Page 42 **less than 1.5 percent:** Mortillaro, Nicole. "Looking Back to Apollo 11: How We Did So Much with So Little." *CBC News*, July 20, 2019. https://www.cbc.ca/news/science/apollo-11-tech-1.5208758.

Page 42 **again until 1981:** Howell, Elizabeth. "How John Young Smuggled a Corned-Beef Sandwich into Space." *Space.com*, January 10, 2018. https://www.space.com/39341-john-young-smuggled-corned-beef-space.html.

Page 43 **on decision-making:** De Smet, Aaron, Gregor Jost, and Leigh Weiss. "Three Keys to Faster, Better Decisions." *McKinsey & Company*, May 1, 2019. https://www.mckinsey.com/capabilities/people-and-organizational-performance/our-insights/three-keys-to-faster-better-decisions.

Aminov, Iskandar, Aaron De Smet, Gregor Jost, and David Mendelsohn. "Decision Making in the Age of Urgency." *McKinsey & Company*, April 30, 2019. https://www.mckinsey.com/capabilities/people-and-organizational-performance/our-insights/decision-making-in-the-age-of-urgency.

Page 44 **food and shelter:** Lieberman, Matthew D. *Social: Why Our Brains Are Wired to Connect*. New York: Broadway Books, 2013.

Page 44 **brains as physical:** Eisenberger, Naomi I., Matthew D. Lieberman, and Kipling D. Williams. "Does Rejection Hurt? An FMRI Study of Social Exclusion." *Science* 302, no. 5643 (October 2003): 290–2. https://pubmed.ncbi.nlm.nih.gov/14551436/.

Page 45 **of diverse thinkers:** Larson, Erik. "New Research: Diversity + Inclusion = Better Decision Making at Work." *Forbes*, September 21, 2017. https://www.forbes.com/sites/eriklarson/2017/09/21/new-research-diversity-inclusion-better-decision-making-at-work/?sh=6ced316a4cbf.

Page 50 **done on time:** Clear, James. *Atomic Habits: An Easy & Proven Way to Build Good Habits & Break Bad Ones.* New York: Avery, 2018.

Page 51 **seven crew members:** Applied Social Psychology (ASP). "How Groupthink Played a Role in the Challenger Disaster." *PSYCH 424 Blog. Penn State.* October 7, 2020. https://sites.psu.edu/aspsy/2020/10/07/how-groupthink-played-a-role-in-the-challenger-disaster/.

Page 51 **comprehensive retroactive study:** U.S. Government Printing Office. *Investigation of the Challenger Accident: Report of the Committee on Science and Technology House of Representatives, Ninety-Ninth Congress, Second Session.* Washington, DC: U.S. Government Printing Office, 1986. https://www.govinfo.gov/content/pkg/GPO-CRPT-99hrpt1016/pdf/GPO-CRPT-99hrpt1016.pdf.

Page 51 **the first place:** Applied Social Psychology (ASP). "How Groupthink Played a Role in the Challenger Disaster." *PSYCH 424 Blog. Penn State. October 7, 2020.* https://sites.psu.edu/aspsy/2020/10/07/how-groupthink-played-a-role-in-the-challenger-disaster/.

U.S. Government Printing Office. *Investigation of the Challenger Accident: Report of the Committee on Science and Technology House of Representatives, Ninety-Ninth Congress, Second Session.* Washington, DC: U.S. Government Printing Office, 1986. https://www.govinfo.gov/content/pkg/GPO-CRPT-99hrpt1016/pdf/GPO-CRPT-99hrpt1016.pdf.

Page 57 **moon landing missions:** "NOVA; To the Moon; Interview with George Mueller, Engineer and Associate Administrator at NASA, Part 3 of 3." 1998, GBH Archives, accessed May 3 2024. https://openvault.wgbh.org/catalog/V_27C413D6CDC84B3E88C46B5E43F30321.

CHAPTER 3: Never Trust a Cheap Lunch: How to Take Back Control of Your Time

Page 62 **that there are:** Casali, Erin 'Folletto.' "'Focusing Is about Saying No' - Steve Jobs (WWDC'97)." YouTube Video, 1:35. June 26, 2011. https://www.youtube.com/watch?v=H8eP99neOVs.

Page 63 **the planning fallacy:** Greene, Jessica. "Why We're Bad at Estimating Time (and What to Do about It)." *Zapier* (Blog). *Zapier.* February 25, 2019. https://zapier.com/blog/how-to-estimate-time/.

Page 65 **because you're overwhelmed:** Newport, Cal. "Engineering Your Workload to Eliminate Stress." YouTube Video. November 9, 2022. https://www.youtube.com/watch?v=TH_xAR7pljU.

Page 66 **decision-making, etc.:** Funahashi, Shintaro. "Prefrontal Contribution to Decision-Making under Free-Choice Conditions." *Frontiers in Neuroscience* 11 (July 2017). https://www.frontiersin.org/journals/neuroscience/articles/10.3389/fnins.2017.00431/full.

Stiedl, Oliver, and Torben Hager. "Cardiovascular Conditioning: Neural Substrates." In *Encyclopedia of Behavioral Neuroscience*, edited by Larry R. Squire, 226-235. Amsterdam: Elsevier Ltd.: Academic Press, 2010.

Page 66 **a novelty bias:** Levitin, Daniel J. "Why the Modern World Is Bad for Your Brain." *The Guardian*, January 18, 2015. https://www.theguardian.com/science/2015/jan/18/modern-world-bad-for-brain-daniel-j-levitin-organized-mind-information-overload.

Page 67 **to prioritize distraction:** Levitin, Daniel J. "Why the Modern World Is Bad for Your Brain." *The Guardian*, January 18, 2015. https://www.theguardian.com/science/2015/jan/18/modern-world-bad-for-brain-daniel-j-levitin-organized-mind-information-overload.

Page 67 **distractions at work:** Web Desk. "How to Focus at Work in the Age of Distractions #Infographic." *Visualistan*, June 2, 2016. https://www.visualistan.com/2016/06/how-to-focus-at-work-in-the-age-of-distractions.html.

Yaqub, Mohammad. "Workplace Distractions Statistics & Trends [2023 Update]." *BusinessDIT*, September 29, 2023. https://www.businessdit.com/distraction-work-statistics/#how-many-hours-per-work-day-are-lost-due-to-distraction.

Page 67 **the word priorities:** Bellis, Mary. "20th Century Invention Timeline 1900 to 1949." *ThoughtCo*, January 24, 2020. https://www.thoughtco.com/20th-century-timeline-1992486.

Page 67 **priority was singular:** Google Books Ngram Viewer. "Priorities, Prioritization." *Google Books*, 2019. https://books.google.com/ngrams/graph?content=priorities%2Cprioritization&year_start=1800&year_end=2019&corpus=en-2019&smoothing=3.

Page 70 **at any time:** Cowan, Nelson. "The Magical Mystery Four: How Is Working Memory Capacity Limited, and Why?" *Current Directions in Psychological Science* 19, no. 1 (February 2010): 51–7. https://www.ncbi.nlm.nih.gov/pmc/articles/PMC2864034/.

Page 73 **you cannot multitask:** Madore, Kevin P., and Anthony D. Wagner. "Multicosts of Multitasking." *Cerebrum* 2019, cer-04-19 (April

2019). https://www.ncbi.nlm.nih.gov/pmc/articles/PMC7075496/.

Page 74 **less work done:** Rubinstein, J. S., D. E. Meyer, and J. E. Evans. "Executive Control of Cognitive Processes in Task Switching." *The Journal of Experimental Psychology: Human Perception and Performance* 27, no. 4 (August 2001): 763–97. https://pubmed.ncbi.nlm.nih. gov/11518143/.

American Psychological Association. "Multitasking: Switching Costs." *American Psychological Association,* March 20, 2006. https://www.apa. org/topics/research/multitasking.

Page 74 **about 10 percent:** Wainwright, Martin. "Emails 'Pose Threat to IQ.'" *The Guardian,* April 22, 2005. https://www.theguardian.com/ technology/2005/apr/22/money.workandcareers.

Griffey, Harriet. "The Lost Art of Concentration: Being Distracted in a Digital World." *The Guardian,* October 14, 2018. https://www. theguardian.com/lifeandstyle/2018/oct/14/the-lost-art-of-concentration-being-distracted-in-a-digital-world.

Bonnie, Emily. 2021. "Addicted to Multitasking: The Scientific Reasons You Can't Stop Juggling Work." *Wrike Blog. Wrike.* July 28, 2021. https://www.wrike.com/blog/addicted-multitasking-scientific-reasons-you-cant-stop-juggling-work/.

Gillette, Hope. "The Average IQ: What It Is and How It's Measured." *PsychCentral,* October 24, 2022. https://psychcentral.com/health/average-iq.

PART 2: UNLOCK

CHAPTER 4: It's Not a Syndrome: How to Promote the Imposter in You

Page 90 **evidence of your success:** Huecker, Martin R., Jacob Shreffler, Patrick T. McKeny, and David Davis. *Imposter Phenomenon.* Florida: StatPearls Publishing, 2024. https://www.ncbi.nlm.nih.gov/books/ NBK585058/.

Merriam-Webster. "Imposter syndrome Definition & Meaning." *Merriam-Webster,* May 2, 2024. https://www.merriam-webster.com/dictionary/impostor%20syndrome.

Page 90 **leads to burnout:** Ravindran, Sandeep. "Feeling Like a Fraud: The Impostor Phenomenon in Science Writing." *The Open Notebook,* November 15, 2016. https://www.theopennotebook.com/2016/11/15/ feeling-like-a-fraud-the-impostor-phenomenon-in-science-writing/.

Page 90 **in their careers:** Abramson, Ashley. "How to Overcome Impostor Phenomenon." *Monitor on Psychology* 52, no. 4 (June 2021): 44. https://www.apa.org/monitor/2021/06/cover-impostor-phenomenon.

Page 90 **she didn't belong:** Clance, Pauline Rose. "Imposter Phenomenon (IP)." *Pauline Rose Clance*, 2013. https://www.paulineroseclance.com/impostor_phenomenon.html.

Page 91 **their initial research:** The Decision Lab. "Imposter Syndrome." *The Decision Lab*, 2024. https://thedecisionlab.com/reference-guide/organizational-behavior/impostor-syndrome.

Page 91 **full-blown imposter syndrome:** Anderson, L.V. "Feeling Like an Imposter Is Not a Syndrome." *Slate*, April 12, 2016. https://slate.com/business/2016/04/is-impostor-syndrome-real-and-does-it-affect-women-more-than-men.html.

Page 91 **Roughly 40 percent:** Baptist Health. "10 Most Common Phobias & Fears." *Baptist Health Blog. Baptist Health.* September 22, 2020. https://www.baptisthealth.com/blog/family-health/10-most-common-phobias-fears.

Page 91 **work every day:** Dubner, Stephen J. "Why Is Flying Safer Than Driving?" *Freakonomics Radio* (podcast). March 1, 2023. Accessed May 2, 2024. https://freakonomics.com/podcast/why-is-flying-safer-than-driving/.

Page 92 **in imposter syndrome:** Tewfik, Basima A. Curriculum Vitae. "Faculty Directory," Sloan School of Management, Massachusetts Institute of Technology. Accessed January 2024. https://mitsloan.mit.edu/shared/ods/documents?PersonID=187610&DocID=11178.

Page 93 **as a syndrome:** Harrell, Eben. "Impostor Syndrome Has Its Advantages." *Harvard Business Review*, May–June 2022. https://hbr.org/2022/05/impostor-syndrome-has-its-advantages.

Page 93 **a training exercise:** Tewfik, Basima A. "The Unexpected Benefits of Doubting Your Own Competence." *Wharton IDEAS Lab*, 2024. https://ideas.wharton.upenn.edu/research/imposter-syndrome-unexpected-benefits/.

Page 93 **more "other-focused":** Tewfik, Basima A. "The Impostor Phenomenon Revisited: Examining the Relationship between Workplace Impostor Thoughts and Interpersonal Effectiveness at Work." *Academy of Management Journal* 65, no. 3 (June 2022): 988–1018. https://journals.aom.org/doi/abs/10.5465/amj.2020.1627?journalCode=amj.

Page 93 **"To date..."**: Harrell, Eben. "Impostor Syndrome Has Its Advantages." *Harvard Business Review,* May–June 2022. https://hbr.org/2022/05/impostor-syndrome-has-its-advantages.

Page 95 **kinds of conversations:** Brooks, Alison Wood, and Leslie K. John. "The Surprising Power of Questions." *Harvard Business Review,* May–June 2018. https://hbr.org/2018/05/the-surprising-power-of-questions.

Page 95 **questions every second:** Mohsin, Maryam. "10 Google Search Statistics You Need to Know in 2023 [Infographic]." *Oberlo* (Blog). *Oberlo.* January 13, 2023. https://www.oberlo.com/blog/google-search-statistics.

Page 96 **building more trust:** Hagel III, John. "Good Leadership Is About Asking Good Questions." *Harvard Business Review,* January 8, 2021. https://hbr.org/2021/01/good-leadership-is-about-asking-good-questions.

Page 96 **and better connections:** Brooks, Alison Wood, and Leslie K. John. "The Surprising Power of Questions." *Harvard Business Review,* May–June 2018. https://hbr.org/2018/05/the-surprising-power-of-questions.

Huang, Karen, Michael Yeomans, Alison Wood Brooks, Julia Minson, and Francesca Gino. "It Doesn't Hurt to Ask: Question-Asking Increases Liking." *Journal of Personality and Social Psychology* 113, no. 3 (2017): 430–52. https://www.hbs.edu/ris/Publication%20Files/Huang%20et%20al%202017_6945bc5e-3b3e-4c0a-addd-254c9e603c60.pdf.

Page 97 **people like you:** Huang, Karen, Michael Yeomans, Alison Wood Brooks, Julia Minson, and Francesca Gino. "It Doesn't Hurt to Ask: Question-Asking Increases Liking." *Journal of Personality and Social Psychology 113, no. 3 (2017): 430–52.* https://www.hbs.edu/ris/Publication%20Files/Huang%20et%20al%202017_6945bc5e-3b3e-4c0a-addd-254c9e603c60.pdf.

CHAPTER 5: My Billion-Dollar Business Mistake: How to Measure Your Joy on the Job

Page 112 **with your colleagues:** Judge, Timothy A., Joyce E. Bono, Amir Erez, and Edwin A Locke. "Core Self-Evaluations and Job and Life Satisfaction: The Role of Self-Concordance and Goal Attainment." *Journal of Applied Psychology* 90, no. 2 (March 2005): 257–68. https://pubmed.ncbi.nlm.nih.gov/15769236/.

Amabile, T. M., S. G. Barsade, J. S. Mueller, and B. M. Staw. "Affect and Creativity at Work." *Administrative Science Quarterly* 50, no. 3 (2005): 367–403. https://journals.sagepub.com/doi/10.2189/asqu.2005.50.3.367.

O'Keefe, Paul A. "Liking Work Really Matters." *New York Times,* September 5, 2014. https://www.nytimes.com/2014/09/07/opinion/sunday/go-with-the-flow.html?_r=0.

O'Keefe, Paul A., and Lisa Linnenbrink-Garcia. "The Role of Interest in Optimizing Performance and Self-Regulation." *Journal of Experimental Social Psychology* 53, (2014): 70-78. https://www.sciencedirect.com/science/article/abs/pii/S002210311400016X.

Pollack, Jeffrey M., Violet T. Ho, Ernest H. O'Boyle, and Bradley L. Kirkman. "Passion at Work: A Meta-Analysis of Individual Work Outcomes." *Journal of Organizational Behaviour* 41, no. 4 (February 2022): 311-331. https://onlinelibrary.wiley.com/doi/10.1002/job.2434.

Kwon, Mijeong, Julia Lee Cunningham, and Jon M. Jachimowicz. "Discerning Saints: Moralization of Intrinsic Motivation and Selective Prosociality at Work." *Academy of Management Journal* 66, no. 6 (December 2023). https://journals.aom.org/doi/abs/10.5465/amj.2020.1761?af=R.

Page 113 **life as well:** Shimazu, Akihito, Wilmar B. Schaufeli, Kimika Kamiyama, and Norito Kawakami. "Workaholism vs. Work Engagement: The Two Different Predictors of Future Well-Being and Performance." *International Journal of Behavioral Medicine* 22, no. 1 (February 2015): 18–23. https://pubmed.ncbi.nlm.nih.gov/24696043/.

Faragher, E. B., M. Cass, and C. L. Cooper. "The Relationship between Job Satisfaction and Health: A Meta-Analysis." *Occupational and Environmental Medicine* 62, no. 2 (February 2005): 105–12. https://pubmed.ncbi.nlm.nih.gov/15657192/.

Page 115 **people feel happier:** Brickman, P., D. Coates, and R. Janoff-Bulman. "Lottery Winners and Accident Victims: Is Happiness Relative?" *Journal of Personality and Social Psychology* 36, no. 8 (August 1978): 917–27. https://pubmed.ncbi.nlm.nih.gov/690806/.

Haupt, Angela. "6 Surprising Things You Think Are Making You Happy—But Are Doing the Opposite." *Time,* January 9, 2023. https://time.com/6240219/things-that-wont-make-you-happy/.

Dahl, Melissa. "A Classic Psychology Study on Why Winning the Lottery Won't Make You Happier." *The Cut,* January 13, 2016. https://www.thecut.com/2016/01/classic-study-on-happiness-and-the-lottery.html.

Page 115 **any meaningful event:** Frederick, Shane and George Loewenstein. "Hedonic Adaptation." In *Well-Being: The Foundations of Hedonic Psychology*, edited by D. Kahneman, E. Diener, and N. Schwarz, 302–329. United States: Russell Sage Foundation, 1999. https://psycnet.apa.org/record/1999-02842-016.

Page 117 **in the past:** Colombo, Desirée, Carlos Suso-Ribera, Javier Fernández-Álvarez, Pietro Cipresso, Azucena Garcia-Palacios, Giuseppe Riva, and Cristina Botella. "Affect Recall Bias: Being Resilient by Distorting Reality." *Cognitive Therapy and Research* 44 (June 2020): 906–18. https://link.springer.com/article/10.1007/s10608-020-10122-3.

Page 118 **almost sixty years:** Prati, Alberto, and Claudia Senik. "Feeling Good Is Feeling Better." *Psychological Science* 33, no. 11 (October 2022): 1828–41. https://journals.sagepub.com/doi/10.1177/09567976221096158.

Page 118 **moment-based human happiness:** Bryson, Alex, and George MacKerron. "Are You Happy While You Work?" *The Economic Journal* 127, no. 599 (April 2015): 106–25. https://www.sole-jole.org/assets/docs/13058.pdf.

MacKerron, George. "Mapping Happiness over Space, Time, & More." November 2017. https://dam.ukdataservice.ac.uk/media/605020/mackerron.pdf.

CHAPTER 6: Don't Unsubscribe from Yourself: How to Unlock More Joy at Your Job

Page 142 **here and now:** Bradt, Steve. "Wandering Mind Not a Happy Mind." *The Harvard Gazette,* November 11, 2010. https://news.harvard.edu/gazette/story/2010/11/wandering-mind-not-a-happy-mind/.

Killingsworth, Matt. "Does Mind-Wandering Make You Unhappy?" *Greater Good Magazine,* July 16, 2013. https://greatergood.berkeley.edu/article/item/does_mind_wandering_make_you_unhappy.

Mrazek, Michael D., Michael S. Franklin, and Jonathan W. Schooler. "Mindfulness Training Improves Working Memory Capacity and GRE Performance While Reducing Mind Wandering." *Psychological Science* 24, no. 5 (March 2013): 776–81. https://journals.sagepub.com/doi/10.1177/0956797612459659.

Colzato, Lorenza S., Ayca Ozturk, Bernhard Hommel. "Meditate to Create: The Impact of Focused-Attention and Open-Monitoring Training on Convergent and Divergent Thinking." *Frontiers in Psychology* 3

(April 2012): 116. https://www.frontiersin.org/journals/psychology/articles/10.3389/fpsyg.2012.00116/full.

Page 142 **feel less happy:** Bradt, Steve. "Wandering Mind Not a Happy Mind." *The Harvard Gazette,* November 11, 2010. https://news.harvard.edu/gazette/story/2010/11/wandering-mind-not-a-happy-mind/.

PART 3: UNLEASH

CHAPTER 7: The World's Best Soccer Prophet: How to Make Better Decisions

Page 151 **about 0.56 percent:** Kowalski, Maciej. "Coin Flip Probability Calculator." *Omni Calculator,* April 8, 2024. https://www.omnicalculator.com/statistics/coin-flip-probability.

Page 151 **you would have won:** McGowan, Tom. "The Life and Times of Paul the Octopus." *CNN,* October 26, 2010. http://edition.cnn.com/2010/SPORT/football/10/26/football.paul.octopus.dies/index.html.

Page 152 **fifteen years later:** Ulmer, Ben, and Matthew Fernandez. "Predicting Soccer Match Results in the English Premier League." Stanford University: School of Computer Science, 2014. https://cs229.stanford.edu/proj2014/Ben%20Ulmer,%20Matt%20Fernandez,%20Predicting%20Soccer%20Results%20in%20the%20English%20Premier%20League.pdf.

Page 154 **25 quadrillion pathways:** LifeXchange. "Neural Pathways: How Your Mind Stores the Info and Thoughts That Affect Your Behaviour." *LifeXchange,* 2024. https://lifexchangesolutions.com/neural-pathways/.

Page 154 **of your energy:** Heid, Markham. "Does Thinking Burn Calories? Here's What the Science Says." *Time,* September 19, 2018. https://time.com/5400025/does-thinking-burn-calories/.

Page 155 **at their faces:** Dolan, Eric W. "Study Reveals Just How Quickly We Form a First Impression." *PsyPost,* October 30, 2017. https://www.psypost.org/study-reveals-just-quickly-form-first-impression/.

Page 156 **think looks best:** Olivola, Christopher, and Alexander Todorov. "The Look of a Winner." *Scientific American,* May 5, 2009. https://www.scientificamerican.com/article/the-look-of-a-winner/.

Antonakis, John, and Olaf Dalgas. "Predicting Elections: Child's Play!" *Science* 323, no. 5918 (February 2009): 1183. https://www.science.org/

doi/10.1126/science.1167748.

Page 156 **identified to date:** Desjardins, Jeff. "24 Cognitive Biases That Are Warping Your Perception of Reality." *World Economic Forum,* November 30, 2021. https://www.weforum.org/agenda/2021/11/humans-cognitive-bias-mistake/.

Heick, Terrell. "The Cognitive Biases List: A Visual of 180+ Heuristics." *Teach Thought,* July 3, 2019. https://www.teachthought.com/critical-thinking/cognitive-biases/.

Page 157 **for combat duty:** McLaughlin, Kevin. "Hire Like the Israeli Military." *Socratic Owl,* November 21, 2016. https://socraticowl.com/post/hire-like-the-israeli-military/.

Page 158 **the algorithm itself:** McLaughlin, Kevin. "Hire Like the Israeli Military." *Socratic Owl,* November 21, 2016. https://socraticowl.com/post/hire-like-the-israeli-military/.

Page 160 **"...dozens of cons":** Iger, Robert. *The Ride of a Lifetime: Lessons Learned from 15 Years as CEO of the Walt Disney Company.* New York: Random House, 2019.

Page 161 **million per film:** The Numbers. "Box Office History for Disney-Pixar Movies." *The Numbers,* 2024. https://www.the-numbers.com/movies/production-company/Pixar.

Page 167 **paper or digital:** Morgenstern, Julie. "The Advantages of Paper VS Digital Planning." *Blog—Julie Morgenstern. Julie Morgenstern Solutions,* 2023. https://www.juliemorgenstern.com/tips-tools-blog/paper-vs-digital-planning.

Codiva, Michelle. "Why Writing on Paper Gives More Ethical Decision Than Doing It on a Digital Device?" *The Science Times,* August 19, 2022. https://www.sciencetimes.com/articles/39463/20220819/decision-making-why-writing-paper-gives-better-answer-doing-digital.htm.

CHAPTER 8: You Bought How Much Toilet Paper? How to Get More Feedback

Page 173 **in total sales:** Shopify. "Shopify Creates the Best Commerce Tools for Anyone, Anywhere, to Start and Grow a Business." *Shopify,* accessed March 2024. https://www.shopify.com/news/company-info.

Page 174 **learn and develop new skills:** Hattie, John, and Helen Timperley. "The Power of Feedback." *Review of Educational Research* 77, no. 1 (March 2007): 81–112. https://www.columbia.edu/~mvp19/ETF/Feedback.pdf.

Page 174 **improves what you're:** Kluger, Avraham N., and Angelo DeNisi. "The Effects of Feedback Interventions on Performance: A Historical Review, a Meta-Analysis, and a Preliminary Feedback Intervention Theory." *Psychological Bulletin* 119, no. 2 (1996): 254–84. https://mrbartonmaths.com/resourcesnew/8.%20Research/Marking%20and%20Feedback/The%20effects%20of%20feedback%20interventions.pdf.

Barends, E., D. Rousseau, E. Wietrak, and I. Cioca. *Performance feedback: An evidence review. Scientific summary.* London: Chartered Institute of Personnel and Development, 2022. https://www.cipd.org/globalassets/media/knowledge/knowledge-hub/evidence-reviews/performance-feedback-scientific-summary_tcm18-111387.pdf.

Liu, Shuwei, Yuchun Xiao, and Xinlai Wang. "How Does Feedback Valence Improve Team Creativity by Influencing Team Relationship Conflict?" *Psychology Research and Behavior Management* 15 (August 2022): 2391-2407. https://www.ncbi.nlm.nih.gov/pmc/articles/PMC9443283/.

Page 174 **your overall motivation:** McLain, Denise, and Bailey Nelson. "How Effective Feedback Fuels Performance." *Gallup,* January 19, 2024. https://www.gallup.com/workplace/357764/fast-feedback-fuels-performance.aspx.

Porath, Christine. "Give Your Team More-Effective Positive Feedback." *Harvard Business Review,* October 25, 2016. https://hbr.org/2016/10/give-your-team-more-effective-positive-feedback.

Page 175 **outperform those without:** Porath, Christine. "Give Your Team More-Effective Positive Feedback." *Harvard Business Review,* October 25, 2016. https://hbr.org/2016/10/ give-your-team-more-effective-positive-feedback.

Page 175 **aren't getting enough:** Richardson, Daniel. "63% of Employees Want More Regular Feedback." *Unleash,* July 27, 2022. https://www.unleash.ai/talent-management/63-of-employees-want-more-regular-feedback/.

Mazur, Caitlin. "20 Essential Employee Feedback Statistics [2023]: Employees Want More Than Just Performance Reviews." *Zippia,* February 1, 2023. https://www.zippia.com/advice/employee-feedback-statistics/.

Mcewan, Victoria. 2023. "Employee Feedback Statistics You Need to Know." *Oak Engage—Blog. Oak Engage.* March 21, 2023. https://www.oak.com/blog/employee-feedback-statistics/.

Page 176 **it would provide:** Abel, Jennifer E., Preeti Vani, Nicole Abi-Es-ber, Hayley Blunden, and Juliana Schroeder. "Kindness in Short Supply: Evidence for Inadequate Prosocial Input." *Current Opinion in Psychology* 48 (December 2022). https://www.sciencedirect.com/science/article/abs/pii/S2352250X22001798?via%3Dihub.

Simon, Lauren S., Christopher C. Rosen, Ravi S. Gajendran, Sibel Oz-gen, and Emily S. Corwin. "Pain or gain? Understanding How Trait Empathy Impacts Leader Effectiveness Following the Provision of Negative Feedback." *Journal of Applied Psychology* 107, no. 2 (February 2022): 279-297. https://pubmed.ncbi.nlm.nih.gov/33829830/.

Moyer, Melinda Wenner. "The Case for Criticism." *New York Times*, April 19, 2022. https://www.nytimes.com/2022/04/14/well/live/constructive-criticism.html.

Page 176 **the supply shortage:** Abi-Esber, Nicole, Jennifer E. Abel, Juli-ana Schroeder, and Francesca Gino. "'Just Letting You Know . . .' Un-derestimating Others' Desire for Constructive Feedback." *Journal of Personality and Social Psychology* 123, no. 6 (December 2022): 1362–85. https://pubmed.ncbi.nlm.nih.gov/35324242/.

Page 178 **over 20 percent:** Strohmetz, David B., Bruce Rind, Reed Fisher, and Michael Lynn. "Sweetening the Till: The Use of Candy to Increase Restaurant Tipping." *Journal of Applied Social Psychology* 32, no. 2 (July 2006): 300–9. https://onlinelibrary.wiley.com/doi/abs/10.1111/j.1559-1816.2002.tb00216.x.

Page 180 **for Creative Leadership:** Leading Effectively Staff. "Use Situation-Behavior-Impact (SBI)™ to Understand Intent." *Center for Creative Leadership*, November 18, 2022. https://www.ccl.org/articles/leading-effectively-articles/closing-the-gap-between-intent-vs-impact-sbii/.

CHAPTER 9: The Impossible 10x Request: How to See Opportunities Everyone Else Misses

Page 196 **you already believe:** Casad, Bettina J., and J.E. Luebering. "Confirmation Bias." *Encyclopedia Britannica*, February 14, 2024. https://www.britannica.com/science/confirmation-bias.

ABOUT THE AUTHOR

Jason Silver is a multi-time founder of kids and a multi-time founder of companies. He gets his biggest thrill helping modern employees and their teams unlock a better way to work—surfing is a close second. He was an early employee at Airbnb and helped build an AI company from the ground up back before AI was the cool thing to do. Today, he advises a startup portfolio valued in the billions on how to build great, lasting companies that people actually enjoy working for. He's a sought-after public speaker, instructor, and advisor on how to transform work into one of the biggest drivers of positivity in your life. When he's not busy helping people solve their hardest workplace challenges, Jason's kids are busy reminding him just how much of a work in progress he still is too.